SpringerBriefs in Sociology

SpringerBriefs in Sociology

SpringerBriefs in Sociology are concise summaries of cutting-edge research and practical applications across the field of sociology. These compact monographs are refereed by and under the editorial supervision of scholars in Sociology or cognate fields. Volumes are 50 to 125 pages (approximately 20,000- 70,000 words), with a clear focus. The series covers a range of content from professional to academic such as snapshots of hot and/or emerging topics, in-depth case studies, and timely reports of state-of-the art analytical techniques. The scope of the series spans the entire field of Sociology, with a view to significantly advance research. The character of the series is international and multi-disciplinary and will include research areas such as: health, medical, intervention studies, cross-cultural studies, race/class/ gender, children, youth, education, work and organizational issues, relationships, religion, ageing, violence, inequality, critical theory, culture, political sociology, social psychology, and so on. Volumes in the series may analyze past, present and/ or future trends, as well as their determinants and consequences. Both solicited and unsolicited manuscripts are considered for publication in this series. SpringerBriefs in Sociology will be of interest to a wide range of individuals, including sociologists, psychologists, economists, philosophers, health researchers, as well as practitioners across the social sciences. Briefs will be published as part of Springer's eBook collection, with millions of users worldwide. In addition, Briefs will be available for individual print and electronic purchase. Briefs are characterized by fast, global electronic dissemination, standard publishing contracts, easy-to-use manuscript preparation and formatting guidelines, and expedited production schedules. We aim for publication 8-12 weeks after acceptance.

Luz Angela Cardona Acuña
Nelson Arteaga Botello

Feminism, Power and Public Opinion in Mexico

Fighting for Civil Repair

 Springer

Luz Angela Cardona Acuña (iD)
Universidad Autónoma de Guerrero
Acapulco, Guerrero, Mexico

Nelson Arteaga Botello (iD)
Facultad Latinoamericana de Ciencias
Sociales-México
Tlalpan, Ciudad de México, Mexico

ISSN 2212-6368   ISSN 2212-6376   (electronic)
SpringerBriefs in Sociology
ISBN 978-3-032-14140-8   ISBN 978-3-032-14141-5   (eBook)
https://doi.org/10.1007/978-3-032-14141-5

This Springer imprint is published by the registered company Springer Nature Switzerland AG
The registered company address is: Gewerbestrasse 11, 6330 Cham, Switzerland

If disposing of this product, please recycle the paper.

Competing Interests The authors have no competing interests to declare that are relevant to the content of this manuscript.

Contents

Chapter 1
Introduction

Abstract This chapter analyzes the relationship between the feminist movement, the disputes within public opinion, and the expressions of presidential power in the face of the mobilizations occurring in the 2020s in Mexico. To do so, we call upon the theory of the civil sphere to help demonstrate how these factors generated a powerful mobilization of public opinion to demand that the president recognize and address the wave of violence against women and femicide. By articulating the supposed demands of the "public" regarding violence against women, those who mobilized exercised their capacity for civil power. However, while a part of the public supported the demands to stop violence, the president declared that its main objective was to destabilize the government and tarnish the presidential investiture, a position supported by many with social power, along with a part of public opinion.

Keywords Feminist mobilization · Presidential power · Mexico · Civil sphere theory · Public opinion · Civil power · Social power

This book shows how four feminist mobilizations, which occurred in the first years of Andrés Manuel López Obrador's administration, triggered a generalized rejection of harassment, sexual violence, and femicide. These mobilizations fostered agreement regarding the urgency of containing violence against women and attending to its victims through a model of prevention, justice, and non-recidivism. At the same time, the dramatizations used in the mobilizations, such as anonymous denunciation and violence against public property, generated a dispute about the legitimacy of the movement. In particular, these mobilizations, as well as others that occurred during Obrador's six-year term—beyond the legitimacy of their demands, were interpreted by the state as actions directed against the presidential figure and the mayor of Mexico City, expressions that sought to weaken what was called the Fourth Transformation of the country.

L. A. Cardona Acuña, N. Arteaga Botello, *Feminism, Power and Public Opinion in Mexico*, SpringerBriefs in Sociology,
https://doi.org/10.1007/978-3-032-14141-5_1

In December 2018, the first self-described leftist candidate became president of the republic of Mexico. Andrés Manuel López Obrador took office, supported by the Movimiento de Renovación Nacional (Morena) party (the National Regeneration Movement Party) and a broad spectrum of progressive social movements and organizations. The president proposed radicalization of the country's democratization process, through a project he called the 4T, or the Fourth Transformation. His discourse followed an anti-elitist, anti-institutional, anti-neoliberal narrative that sought to strengthen the idea of community, horizontality, and plebiscitary expressions of the popular. In this sense, López Obrador activated a narrative of "us," representing the spirit of the 4T, versus "them," namely, those that embrace conservative and reactionary values. The former was characterized by their apparent commitment to the principles of civil virtue and democratic purity, attachment to the people, austerity, and pretensions of social transformation. The latter were characterized as embodying the principles of civil vice, conservatives committed to the political and social elites, tainted by their moral impurity, seeking political and economic gain.

Four days after López Obrador was sworn in as president, Claudia Sheinbaum (also from Morena) took office as the mayor of Mexico City, the nation's capital. Sheinbaum was an ally of the president and his movement, but her political activity dated back to the mid-1980s, as a student leader and a militant of different leftist parties and progressive movements. The careers of López Obrador and Sheinbaum ran along the same path. When López Obrador was mayor of Mexico City between 2006 and 2012, Sheinbaum was his secretary of the environment. At the end of her term, Sheinbaum returned to academic life at the National Autonomous University of Mexico but continued to be a prominent militant in the Party of the Democratic Revolution, in which López Obrador was also a militant. When the latter founded Morena, Sheinbaum followed him in his party project. With the support of MORENA, she became the head of the Tlalpan delegation (2014–2018) and, subsequently, the mayor of Mexico City (2018–2023). In 2023, she was designated as Morena's candidate for the presidency of the republic, acceding to the position in 2024 as the first woman to hold the office.

Sheinbaum's run for the presidency manifested with the clear support of López Obrador, who had reactivated the presidential figure as the main axis for functioning of the regime, with a disciplined and neo-corporate political apparatus through which he exercised his power for 6 years (Arteaga, 2024). During his government, López Obrador operated as a referent that embodied the centralization of political power as a source of meaning for the symbolic framework of national politics. Therefore, the criticisms leveled at his closest political circle—particularly Sheinbaum—were interpreted by López Obrador as attacks on his person and his presidential investiture. In the same vein, political and social mobilization on human rights, missing persons, or violence against women was interpreted as derailing the 4T project.[1]

The feminist mobilizations regarding violence against women and femicide analyzed in this book occurred mainly in Mexico City. They were interpreted by both the official apparatus and certain sectors of public opinion as mobilizations aimed at delegitimizing López Obrador and his political project. His response, along with that of Sheinbaum, was assessed as contrary to what was expected from these leftist leaders and from social movements. Both leveled accusations that the mobilizations were being manipulated by right-wing and conservative groups, actors that sought to undermine the 4T project and its primary representatives.

The Mexican feminist mobilizations followed the pattern of the international #MeToo (#MT) movement on social networks. Thus, men from different areas of social life were exposed as alleged harassers or abusers. The #MT goal was to expose the abuse by men embedded in political, cultural or educational spheres who had used their power to harass or rape women. Unfortunately, the mobilization subsided when a well-known Mexican musician committed suicide after being denounced for allegedly harassing a teenage girl twenty years earlier. This incident produced a barrage of criticism led to the closure of the movement's social networks.

Parallel to the #MeToo feminist mobilizations, violence against women had apparently increased and so did the feeling that there was a social crisis looming. In August 2019, a group of feminists—the Witches of the Sea—called for a protest march under the name #NoMeCiudanMeViolan (#NMCMV)—#TheyDon'tTakeCa reofMeTheyRapeMe. The protest denounced the lack of attention and response from authorities to cases of violence against women perpetrated by the Mexico City police. During the march, monuments were graffitied, and bus stations and police offices were destroyed. This activity sparked a public controversy. The events were criticized by the president and the mayor of Mexico City, who pointed out that the women who protested were not really feminists and instead had the agenda of eroding the legitimacy of the MORENA government.

Violence against women and femicide also prompted a group of feminists to call for a national women's strike under the name #UnDíaSinNosotras (#UDSN)—#ADayWithoutUs, held in March 2020. The president questioned the legitimacy of the call. While he considered the demands of such mobilizations fair, he believed their main objective was to destabilize and generate a "soft coup d'état." These statements engendered voices for and against the president within public opinion. Despite the controversies, some women answered the call for a strike. After this protest, the #MT gained renewed strength. For example, the appointment of one of men closest to the president, who was accused of sexual harassment at an institution of higher education, was rejected. The digital mobilization of #MeToo was perhaps

---

[1] As I elaborate below, the questioning of Sheinbaum's performance as the head of the government in the face of feminist mobilizations was interpreted as direct criticism of President López Obrador, who had ended up appointing -in the old style of patrimonial politics- Sheinbaum as his successor in 2023 (Arteaga, 2024).

one of the possible reasons the president was motivated to abandon the appointment of his former collaborator.

In this book, we analyze the relationship between the feminist movement, the disputes within public opinion, and the expressions of presidential power in the face of the mobilizations occurring in the 2020s in Mexico. To do so, we call upon the theory of the civil sphere to help demonstrate how these factors generated a powerful mobilization of public opinion to demand that the president recognize and address the wave of violence against women and femicide. We also examine how #MT, #NMCMV, and #UDSN sought to speak on behalf of women and expressed the need for immediate action by the president and the mayor of Mexico City. By articulating the supposed demands of the "public" regarding violence against women, those who mobilized exercised their capacity for civil power. However, while a part of the public supported the demands to stop violence, the president declared that its main objective was to destabilize the government and tarnish the presidential investiture, a position supported by many with social power, along with a part of public opinion.

The idea that there exists such a thing known as "public opinion" is embedded in the structure of sentiments in a society, and through it, social actors try to influence institutions by speaking the language of civil discourse. Different opinions can be found in the public sphere because different groups make an effort to translate their interests and ideals into terms of the civic cultural structure. From this perspective, public opinion cannot be seen simply as the result of the imposition of a set of narrow interests or individual worldviews, but rather as a mediator between "the broad binaries of civil society discourse and the institutional domains of social life" (Alexander, 2006, p. 75). In the competition to control the meaning of feminist mobilizations in Mexico, one can observe how the media and authorities spoke to public opinion by idealizing or demonizing them. However, in this game of attributions, the authorities—and the president in particular—end up being demonized, demanding that they recognize the civil nature of feminist mobilizations. This scenario represents an example of how public opinion has the capacity to question any deviations from the civil ideal of the person who embodied the office of president at that time.

The analyses of the women's mobilizations discussed in this book have thus far been approached mainly from the theory of containment repertoires (Rovira-Sancho, 2021; Mandujano-Salazar & Becerra-Soria, 2020; Acosta-Sierra & Corrales-Caro, 2022; Pfleger, 2021; García-González, 2021), frame analysis (Santillana, 2024), studies of resistance (Mingo, 2020; Edmé, 2020; Cerva, 2020), as expressions of political struggle (Álvarez Enríquez, 2020) or collective action (Monsalve et al., 2024), and even as momentary explosions lacking transformative capacity (Ramírez-Arce, 2022). These mobilizations have also been analyzed as expressions of the crisis of the capitalist democratic system, which lacks the capacity to generate mechanisms for feminist representation (Andrade, 2020). Studies that focus on the tense relationship between López Obrador's government and the various women's movements studied in this book tended to explain the tension through the fact that populism is incompatible with feminist demands for autonomy and equality (Beer, 2021), or the idea that there was a confrontation between the official history of women in society and the feminist memory sedimented over the years (Velázquez, 2022), one in which a masculine and exclusionary citizenship (Bolaños & Sánchez, 2022) worked to postpone, disqualify, and repress feminist demands (Sánchez & Velázquez, 2022). Some scholarly work has pointed out that the confrontation between López Obrador and the women's mobilizations ended up weakening the legitimacy of his government (Sánchez-Gudiño, 2022), while others have suggested that it was rather the feminist movement in Mexico that was weakened by the popular support received by the president of the republic (Melgar & Tinat, 2023).

Our research seeks to situate the gaze of #MT, #NMCMV, and #UDSN differently. Existing scholarly work has emphasized that mobilizations respond to the pressures of social externality, violence, and femicide. Reed (2011) suggests that this type of interpretation emplaces meaning and action as soft variables explained as by-products of hard variables such as violence or heteropatriarchy, for example. Taking into account non-patriarchal ideals, gender theory has moved directly from the political macro-truth to its personal micro-effects, often casting aside the ways in which social actors create culturally structured meanings that translate forms of injustice (Broch, 2020). From a gender perspective, violence and femicide trigger protests and mobilizations among women—feminist or not—in an automatic, strategic, and rational way. This perspective sheds little light on how the meanings that account for the relevance of these acts of violence and death are culturally constructed. Intersectional perspectives, although they have made it possible to reveal the complex structures of inequality, continue to privilege structural conditions over the construction of the social actors' meanings (Bloch, 1993).

Critical gender sociology, which links gender with feminist theory, also assumes the existence of a universal gender reality in social life, in which men are the ones who hold power and shape knowledge about masculinities and femininities (Broch, 2020). Once again, patriarchal structures appear omniscient and omnipresent, dominating the entire horizon of the construction of social meaning. This type of perspective is not wrong per se, but it underlines elements that we do not privilege in this study. We assume that to the extent that other interpretations can account for the processes of inequality and conflict in a society in relation to feminist mobilization, it is appropriate to expand beyond a single view. Thus, "while cultural sociology explores how codes, symbols and narrative enable the creation of meaning, the gender perspective emphasizes how social relations of power constrain symbols, narrative and meaning" (Broch, 2020, p. 6).[2]

To understand #MT, the #NMCMV, and the #UDSN, it is necessary to account for the cultural environment that allows violence and femicide to be interpreted as a serious situation, to the point that the authority of presidential power is questioned

---

[2]Certainly, other works, such as those of Fraser (1992) and Seyla Benhabib (1992), emphasize cultural elements, claiming that feminist movements are defined by identity processes, but again, they omit the fact that this is only possible by refracting the universal representations of the civil sphere.

and mobilizes in its favor and against it within public opinion. It is also relevant to account for how public opinion translates feminist mobilizations positively or negatively from the same cultural environment provided by civil discourse. The disputes we analyze in this text are important because they allow us to appreciate how the binary coding of civil/anti-civil attributed to both presidential power and feminist mobilizations reproduced within public opinion is translated into referents assumed as universals of contamination and purification of action. Therefore, public opinion is the condition of intelligibility for criticism or support of presidential power and the demand for civil redress for women subjected to violence. If we want to promote significant changes that allow for the expansion of solidarity and social inclusion, it is necessary to appreciate precisely how these translations are made. In this way, "economic causes" or "heteropatriarchal structures" only acquire meaning if public opinion considers them a relevant political element of symbolic dispute and controversy in society in terms of the civil/anti-civil binary.

Of course, there are positions such as Pateman's (1988), diametrically opposed to the stance taken in this book, insofar as he considers civilian values as immutably patriarchal values. On this point, there is no complementarity between that type of analysis and the one we carry out in this book. We consider that such divergent points as Pateman's (1988) do not lead to a productive communication process; rather, they produce a kind of academic solipsism.[3] Thus, we propose to see feminist mobilizations and their relationship with presidential power and public opinion as a process of meaning making, in which the discourse of civil society makes it possible to translate and also block exceptions to civil redress in the face of violence against women and femicide. This process is interpreted and signified in the light of historical sedimentations, which we believe can complement gender and feminist points of view.

We begin by examining the theory of the civil sphere in Chap. 2, which serves as the framework for analyzing feminist movements in Mexico. It explores how feminist demands have been articulated within the binary classification system prevalent in civil discourse. Chapter 3 analyzes the competition for meaning generated by the conflicting positionings of *#Metoo* and *Autre Parole* (*Another Word*) in 2018 at the international level—in relation to the harassment of female actors and show business personalities—and their repercussions in Ibero-America, Europe, and the United States. Here, we analyze how the competing discourses legitimized and contaminated definitions of what and who the harassers are, at the same time as who the victims are, in terms of civil discourse. We explore how civil and anti-civil motives,

---

[3] This book stands in a different place from theories of collective action (Melucci 1980, 1991, 1999), social conflict (Touraine, 1985), resource mobilization (McCarthy & Mayer, 1977); political opportunity structure (Kitschelt, 1986; Tarrow 1999; McAdam, 1999); framing (Snow et al., 1986); new social movements (Melucci, 1980); collective identities (Polletta & Jasper, 2001); or legal opportunities (Burstein, 1991 and Hilson, 2002). Such theories are focused on a utilitarian line that sees culture as a tool that actors use for their strategic calculations. In this way, the sociological reference to social meanings disappears in favor of attention to external material conditions (Alexander, 2021).

relations, and institutions have been imputed to both *#MeToo* and *Autre Parole*. This exploration allows us to see how, on a global scale, the forms of attribution of civil discourse play a central role in defining the legitimacy of one or another movement's positioning The competing discourses define a symbolic dispute regarding civil redress for acts of violence and harassment towards women, as well as differentiated interpretations of their rights, equality, and gender equity.

In Chap. 4, we look at the #MT movement in terms of public opinion, which questioned presidential power when López Obrador appointed an alleged harasser as Mexico's ambassador to Panama. The #MT movement had demonstrated clear strength, to the point that the Panamanian foreign minister rejected the president's appointment, and Obrador had to withdraw his proposal. This action reveals the scope and the strength of the civil discourse classification system at the regional level. This case is compelling because it highlights how the #MT movement faced serious questioning when an alleged link was established between it and the suicide of a musician accused of harassment. The controversy opened a debate on the relevance of anonymous reports of harassment, and the legal, social, and personal implications, both for the victims and the accused. The movement had been interpreted in the media as an expression of legitimate justice, albeit tainted by rancor and revenge. Some voices among the public considered that the #MT complaints sought only to engage in digital lynching of alleged harassers. The scramble to assign causation to #MT in the musician's suicide apparently weakened the digital harassment allegations. However, it regained strength by questioning the president's appointment of the Mexican ambassador to Panama.

Next, in Chap. 5, we offer an analysis of how feminist and women's mobilization moved from denunciation to action under the #NMCMV banner. Here, we examine how two competing discourses contested the movement's meaning, as well as its consequences in the construction of social inclusion for women. On the one hand, a discourse was developed that considered the acts of protest and "vandalism" among the demonstrators as the expression of their weariness and tiredness in the face of apathy on the part of the authorities; in this way, violence was considered a civil irruption to transform the public life of the city. On the other hand, a discourse was constructed that judged as inappropriate the use of violence by the #NMCMV in 2019, because it exposed a mobilization not only trapped in emotion and irrationality, but also aimed at destabilizing both presidential power and that of the mayor of Mexico City. Our central argument in this chapter is that the dispute over the meaning of the #NMCMV emerged in the form of two competing narratives: one that sought to attribute a pure or civil character to the women who participated in it, thereby underlining their capacity to generate more universal and supportive inclusion, and another narrative that sought to contaminate and highlight the anti-civil profile of the mobilization, with its lack of proposals for solidarity and inclusion.

Chapter 6 explores the dispute over the meaning of the National Women's Strike (#UDSN) in 2020. From one side, it was interpreted as a proposal for autonomous women to make visible the conditions of violence perpetrated against them. From the other, it was seen as an initiative by conservative groups to undermine the legitimacy of the government. Each discourse attributed a civil and anti-civil character to the strike and the social actors supporting it. In the chapter, we show how presidential power and public opinion sought to symbolically control the legitimate or illegitimate character of the #UDSN in relation to certain codes of solidarity and social inclusion. The strike was considered an authentic expression of feminist collectives and independent women, as civil individuals, fed up with the increase in femicide. However, the #UDSN was also judged as inauthentic, with (anti-civil) conservative groups seeking to undermine the legitimacy of the presidency.

The four moments captured in this book allow us to account for how, within public opinion, there is competition to define the symbolic contours of feminism, about who should or should not be considered an authentic or inauthentic feminist, in relation to social and presidential power. In a particular way, the confrontation of narratives between *#MeToo* and *Autre Parole* represented an effort to establish a definition of "harassment" in relationships established by powerful men, who embodied firmly established social power, with women. The relationships often fell into the sphere of spectacle, with the validity of the women's denunciations resonating on a global scale and transversely crossing society. In the case of the movement in Mexico under the banner of #MT, there was a concerted effort on the part of both feminists and the public to define limits on the relevance of anonymous denunciations. Denunciations further brought about debate on the role of presidential power in the face of violence against women. Presidential power served as a change box that sought to establish at what point one could speak of harassment and who could or could not be considered authentic feminists. In the case of #NMCMV and #UDSN, the weight of presidential power in public opinion further marked its strength in establishing narratives that assigned the attributes of the pure or impure feminist. In the end, this book allows us to observe how demands for civil redress by feminists and women activists not only had to confront the traditional pitfalls imposed on them as anti-civil subjects but also faced the consequences when presidential power comes into play.[4]

References

Acosta-Sierra, P. H. & Corrales-Caro, D. A. (2022). Repertoires of resistance and places of memory in social revolt. *Pensamiento palabra y obra,* (28). Advance online publication. https://doi. org/10.17227/ppo.num28-17317

Alexander, J. (2006). *The civil sphere.* Oxford University Press.

Alexander, J. (2021). Introduction: Populism continuum from within the civil sphere to outside it. In J. Alexander, G. Sciortino, & P. Kivisto (Eds.), *Populism in the civil sphere* (pp. 96–124). Polity Press.

Álvarez Enríquez, L. (2020). The feminist movement in Mexico in the 21st century: youth, radicalism and violence. *Revista mexicana de ciencias políticas y sociales, 65*(240), 147–175.

Andrade, V. M. (2020). Problems of legitimation in global capitalism. *Sociológica (Mexico), 35*(100), 45–80.

---

[4] The authors thank Cesar Hurtado Banda for his assistance and support in conducting this research.

Arteaga, N. (2024). *The civil sphere and the semantics of political dispute*. FLACSO Mexico.

Beer, C. (2021). Contradictions and conflict between the Fourth Transformation and the feminist movement. *Politics and Government, 28*(2), 9–18.

Benhabib, S. (1992). *Situating the self: Gender, community, and postmodernism in contemporary ethics*. Routledge.

Bloch, R. (1993). A culturalist critique of trends in feminist theory. *Contention, 2*, 79–106.

Bolaños, Y. B., & Sánchez, C. E. (2022). The "incorrect feminism". El 8M del 2020 en el discurso de Andrés Manuel López Obrador. *LOGOS Revista De Filosofía, 139*(139), 101–118. https://doi.org/10.26457/lrf.v139i139.3350

Broch, T. B. (2020). *A performative feel for the game*. Palgrave Macmillan.

Burstein, P. (1991). Legal mobilization as a social movement tactic: The struggle for equal employment opportunity. *American Journal of Sociology, 98*, 1201–1225.

Cerva, D. C. (2020). Feminist protest in Mexico. Misogyny in institutional discourse and sociodigital networks. *Revista Mexicana de Ciencias Políticas y Sociales, 65*(240), 177–205.

Edmé, D. R. (2020). Mexico and Latin America: From# MeToo to# NiUnaMenos. In G. Chandra & I. Erlingsdóttir (Eds.), *The Routledge handbook of the politics of the# MeToo movement* (pp. 423–438). Routledge.

Fraser, N. (1992). Rethinking the public sphere: A contribution to of actually existing democracy. In C. Calhoun (Ed.), *Habermas and the Public Sphere* (pp. 109–142). MIT.

García-González, L. Ã. (2021). Feminist movements in Mexico: Digital communicative practices and risks. *Virtualis, 12*(23), 44–66.

Hilson, C. (2002). New social movements: The role of legal opportunity. *Journal of European Public Policy, 9*, 238–255.

Kitschelt, H. (1986). Political opportunity structures and political protest: Anti-nuclear movements in four democracies. *British Journal of Political Science, 16*, 57–85.

Mandujano-Salazar, Y. Y., & Becerra-Soria, L. A. (2020). Social media as an instrument of activism for feminist university students in Mexico. In D. Ramírez Plascencia, B. Carvalho Gurgel & A. Plaw (Coords.), *The politics of technology in Latin America (Volume 2): Digital media, daily life and public engagement*, (pp. 81–95). Universidad de Guadalajara.

McAdam, D. (1999). Political opportunities: Terminological origins, current issues, and future lines of research. In D. McAdam, J. D. McCarthy, & M. N. Zald (Eds.), *Social movements: Comparative perspectives* (pp. 49–70). Istmo.

McCarthy, J., & Mayer, Z. (1977). Resource mobilization and social movements: A partial theory. *American Journal of Sociology, 82*, 1212–1242.

Melgar, L., & Tinat, K. (2023). Four years of setbacks and resistance: Women and the feminist movement in the face of the López Obrador government. *Cahiers des Amériques latines, 104*.

Melucci, A. (1980). The new social movements: A theoretical approach. *Social Science Information, 19*, 199–226.

Melucci, A. (1991). Collective action as social construction. *Sociological Studies IX, 26*, 357–364.

Melucci, A. (1999). *Acción Colectiva, vida cotidiana y democracia*. El Colegio de México.

Mingo, A. (2020). "With our voices!": The feminist student struggle against violence. *Journal of Higher Education, 49*(195), 1–20.

Monsalve, L. F. D., Gómez, V. M., Giraldo, E. R. R., Piedrahita, M. A. J., & Arango, B. C. C. (2024). Sexual harassment in university contexts: Review of research between 2006 and 2020. *Journal of Higher Education, 53*(209), 37–58.

Pateman, C. (1988). The fraternal social contract. In J. Keane (Ed.), *Civil society and the state: New European perspectives* (pp. 101–128). Verso.

Pfleger, S. (2021). Strong, free, rebellious. Towards a more agentive identity of the feminist movement in Mexico. *Millcayac: Revista Digital de Ciencias Sociales, 8*(14), 325–348.

Polletta, F., & Jasper, J. (2001). Collective identity and social movements. *Annual Review of Sociology, 27*, 283–305.

Ramírez-Arce, A. (2022). Me Too: A movement or a moment? (pre)conditions, (dis) equalities and social demands. *Estudios Journal*. https://doi.org/10.15517/re.v0i0.51858

Reed, I. A. (2011). *Interpretation and social knowledge: On the use of theory in the human sciences*. University of Chicago Press.

Rovira-Sancho, G. (2021). Activism and affective labor for digital direct action: The Mexican #MeToo campaign. *Social Movement Studies, 22*(2), 145–162. https://doi.org/10.1080/1474283 7.2021.2010530

Sánchez, P. E., & Velázquez, M. A. (2022). Governance in the times of the 4T: The feminist movement and the public agenda. *Intersticios Sociales, 24*, 67–96.

Sánchez-Gudiño, H. (2022). Youth hoods (anarchists and feminists): Crossword puzzle for AMLO's political communication. *Politics, Globality and Citizenship, 8*(16), 287–301.

Santillana, M. (2024). Framing feminist protest: A content analysis of the glitter revolution. *Feminist Media Studies*, 1–17. https://doi.org/10.1080/14680777.2024.2418378

Snow, D., Burke, R., Worden, S., & Benford, R. (1986). Frame alignment processes, micromobilization, and movement participation. *American Sociological Review, 51*, 464–481.

Tarrow, S. (1999). State and opportunity: The political structuring of social movements. In D. McAdam, J. D. McCarthy, & M. N. Zald (Eds.), *Social movements: Comparative perspectives* (pp. 71–99). Istmo.

Touraine, A. (1985). An introduction to the study of social movements. *Social Research: An International Quarterly, 54*, 49–787.

Velázquez, M. M. (2022). Feminist movement versus androcentric state. A dispute between history and memory in Mexico. *Revista Temas Sociológicos, 30*, 419–460.

Chapter 2
The Feminist Movement and the Civil Sphere

Abstract The theoretical foundations of cultural sociology and civil sphere theory suggest that a deep cultural structure gives the civil sphere its significance. This analysis uses concepts such as public opinion and regulatory and communicative institutions to explore how the boundaries of inclusion and exclusion shift in response to demands for justice or civil reparation. It explains the role of social movements as collective actions aimed at articulating demands for civil redress, specifically when addressing particular interpretations of harm or offense in social and moral contexts. Ultimately, the analysis demonstrates that structural hermeneutics is the most effective method for examining journalistic texts, as these texts encapsulate the cultural structures that underlie the movements' demands.

Keywords Public opinion · Communication institutions · Regulatory institutions · Feminist movements · Digital mobilization

2.1 Communicative and Regulative Institutions

Societies have a civil sphere, that is, an institutional and cultural network distinct and relatively autonomous from non-civil institutions such as the state, the market, the family and religion (Alexander, 2006). The civil sphere is a network of discourses and narratives underpinned by symbolic referents that classify social groups, relationships, motives and institutions as falling on either side of a civil/anti-civil binary. Groups may be comprised of rational or irrational, autonomous or heteronomous actors; with open or closed, deliberative or conspiratorial relationships; that build inclusive or exclusive, egalitarian or hierarchical institutions. From this perspective, "'public opinion' refers to the civil and anti-civil evaluations that members of society have about certain groups, their social relations, and in

L. A. Cardona Acuña, N. Arteaga Botello, *Feminism, Power and Public Opinion in Mexico*, SpringerBriefs in Sociology,
https://doi.org/10.1007/978-3-032-14141-5_2

particular about their representative figures or institutions" (Sachs & Alexander, 2023, p. 25). Thus, the normative character of the "public" is constructed through civil discourse.

Social actors are interpreted as being supported by democratic motives if they are believed to be autonomous, rational, reasonable, and realistic, or conversely, by anti-democratic motives if they are judged to lack autonomy, to be irrational and non-realistic. When evaluating relationships among social actors, they are evaluated as civil if they are open, trustworthy, susceptible to criticism, honorable and reliable, and anti-civil if they are evaluated as closed, suspicious, deferential, selfish, or deceitful. Finally, institutions are qualified as civil if they are interpreted as being regulated by law, equitable, inclusive, and impersonal; they are anti-civil if they are evaluated as functioning arbitrarily, hierarchically, exclusionary and for the benefit of one person or group.

The theory of the civil sphere makes it possible to understand the tense relationship between the universal referents of solidarity and inclusion versus the particularistic demands of social groups.[1] This theory recognizes that actors have different interpretations of how solidarity should be crystallized, repeatedly expressing their disagreement on how individual demands and collective obligations are articulated. The disagreement is expressed through imputing attributions of democratic purity and impurity, typifying who deserves to be considered within the fold of inclusion and collective solidarity. The pure or impure character attributed to the actors is relational: "Just as there is no developed religion that does not divide the world between the saved and the damned, there is no civil discourse that does not conceptualize the world between those who deserve inclusion and those who do not" (Alexander, 2006, p. 55).

These imputations are transferred to the communicative and regulatory institutions of the civil sphere, constantly accused of being or not being sufficiently democratic and inclusive.[2] Communicative institutions reflect and disseminate the positions, passions, and interests of those who assume themselves to be part of a society, who speak on behalf of society, towards society, and as society. Examples include the media or voluntary associations and public opinion polls. Regulatory institutions are those that, in the face of social demands for solidarity, can make binding decisions, as is the case with elected officials or courts. On most occasions, class, race, or gender serve as a reference for establishing the degree of integrity or contamination of the actors, their relationships, or their institutions (Kivisto & Sciortino, 2015).

---

[1] As part of the strong program in cultural sociology, civil sphere theory assumes the relative autonomy of the production of meaning. Following Geertz, the interpretations of social actors and the cultural structures on which they depend are the focus of the strong program, not the mechanisms and causes that other approaches assume are behind the actors (Alexander & Smith, 2003).

[2] Authors such as Dagnino et al. (2006) assume a civil society determined by political and ideological projects, defined by its position vis-à-vis the state and the economy. Our analysis assumes the relative autonomy of a civil sphere that reflects the different interpretations of social actors and a cultural structure that helps to understand these disputes.

The theory of the civil sphere posits that public opinion is a symbolic representation that crystallizes "the public" in the collective imagination as if it were a structure of feelings. Actors appeal to public opinion as a normative referent of civil society discourse (Alexander, 2006). Who is democratic, who has broken public morality, which institutions are incapable of generating dynamics of inclusion and solidarity, are questions that are answered in the arena of public opinion. Here, we "mediate between the broad binaries of civil society discourse and the institutional domains of social life. Public opinion is the sea in which we swim, the structure that gives us the feel of democratic life" (Alexander, 2006, p. 75). There is never full agreement within public opinion, because the socially constructed meaning of solidarity and exclusion varies according to the imputations, civil or anti-civil, that social actors make regarding each other.

The media, consisting of the press, television news, and digital media, interpret social actors, their motives, relationships, and institutions. In this way, attributes of civil virtue or civil vice are imputed, and public opinion interprets news and opinion columns as authentic or inauthentic and thereby defines the imputations made about social actors as true or false (Lin, 2019). For their part, surveys construct a representation of social issues and actors within public opinion. The results of a survey generate the feeling that the opinion of the population can be measured and expressed in numbers (Mast, 2006). They also make it possible to draw the asymmetries of positions in society. The results of surveys are regularly judged as the "objective" expression of the collectivity. Surveys, as Alexander (2006) puts it, do not only show public opinion, but also construct it, disrupting the attitudes of society. However, the questions asked in surveys only reflect the system of purity and impurity already contained in social discourses and narratives (Choi, 2019). Pollsters "ask the questions not about the public's opinion in an open-ended meaning, but about what the public wants to know about a situation that has already been communicatively constructed with reference to the binaries of the civil sphere" (Alexander, 2006, p. 87).

Civil associations are groups organized outside the church, the family, or businesses in order to express specific positions on issues of interest to the public. What characterizes these associations is their communicative intent on facts considered relevant to civil society, such as a policy developed by the government, for example (Alexander, 2006). These associations translate binary civil codes into specific claims and demands for the defense of rights, challenging a particular value system or calling for unity and solidarity in the face of an event considered socially traumatic. Some associations operate as spokespersons for social movements. From the perspective of civil sphere theory, social movements are considered mechanisms that allow the translation of disputes over inclusion, solidarity, and civil redress (Alexander, 2006; see also Eyerman & Jamison, 1990). Movements may engender support, as well as counter-responses that seek to maintain the normative interpretation of forms of solidarity and their institutions. By framing their demands in civil terms, civil associations express their intention to expand civil inclusion directly to the public.

2.2   The Civil Sphere and Social Movements

Civil sphere theory conceptualizes social mobilizations as collective actions that seek to translate demands for civil redress in the face of a particular meaning of harm or offense in social and moral terms. Consequently, they always express and mobilize particularistic demands, but always through universal referents of inclusion and solidarity. As expressions of the universal, social movements see themselves as actors that "represent" society, wielding a language that speaks directly to society through the need to expand inclusive membership. They mobilize to generate changes in laws, public policies, and institutions or to call attention to the behavior of officials and politicians. In this order of ideas, feminist mobilizations have transformed the structures of heteropatriarchal domination through the collective action of discourses that signify the conditions of oppression, discrimination, and violence against women (Cardona and Arteaga, 2020). Thus, they push for the construction of civil redress mechanisms that allow for inclusion, equality, and justice (Luengo, 2018, p. 39). The feminist movement has rewritten the relationship between universal values and particularist values of social inclusion (Alexander, 2019).[3] However, in the face of feminist demands, the responses within public opinion have been for and against, generating a communicative dispute about the validity of their demands.

Communicative disputes crystallize in terms of social norms and regulations in the regulative institutions of the civil sphere (Shimizu, 2019). These cannot be confused with institutions of the state (Kivisto & Sciortino, 2019), because state institutions exercise, formally and explicitly, social control by means of legal authority and even the use of violence (Tognato, 2021). The bureaucratic organization of the modern state ensures that governmental decisions are implemented thanks to its ability to coordinate tasks and the definition of objectives. However, Weber (1979) himself warned that the tip of this structure is under the control and direction of forces outside the state, namely, non-bureaucratic power that permanently seeks to make the bureaucratic work operate according to its own interests. In democratic societies, this power is manifested through the vote. Voting is the civil power that largely regulates the bureaucratic order of the state. Unlike the social power that political, business or ecclesiastical elites have, civil power decides who should occupy the highest non-bureaucratic place in the state. It is therefore.

> solidarity translated into governmental control [...] To the extent that there is an independent civil sphere, the people 'speak' not only through the *communicative* institutions that

---

[3] The first and second waves of feminism can be interpreted from the theory of the civil sphere as a first civil reparation effort to modify the status of women in the face of patriarchy, which had built a wall between private and public worlds. It was a cultural effort to redefine the status of what it meant to be a woman: able to make rational decisions and therefore, able to vote, autonomous and therefore able to access property, honest and getting a voice in public decisions, and strong, with the right to work outside the home– (Alexander, 2006; Sachs & Alexander, 2023). The third and fourth waves also put at the center of the discussion new forms of translation and civil reparation of the mechanisms of injustice generated by heteropatriarchy.

give cultural authority but also through the *regulative* institutions. The civil community regulates access to state power. To make this possible, it constitutes a new and different kind of power of its own. To the extent that society is democratic, the regulative institutions are the guardians of political power. It is civil power that opens and closes the door (Alexander, 2006, p. 110).

Civil power is constantly confronted by social power through the regulative institutions of voting, political parties, electoral campaigns, civil service positions, and the law (Thumala, 2018; Villegas, 2019). One of the most powerful regulatory mechanisms in democracies consists of electoral campaigns that culminate in the suffrage of the citizenry. By casting votes at the ballot box, society condenses its feelings about political and social life at a given time. As Mast (2019) suggests, in campaigns, state institutions are staged, monitored, guided, and even challenged by civil organizations, media, and legal institutions. Thus, by voting, one candidate is chosen over another in the belief that they will translate their particular vision of the public good into reality. Once someone comes to power, for example, through the presidency of a country, the case we are interested in here, they must submit to the rules of public office. From this perspective, the rules of public office are considered a regulative institution "that institutionalizes a universalist understanding of the organization of authority" (Alexander, 2006, p. 133).

Thus, upon gaining access to presidential power, individuals are subject to the control mechanisms of civilian power through a regulatory framework that allows either moral sanctions or administrative and criminal punishment for those who have betrayed the universalist conception of authority. Rarely—except in cases of *impeachment*—are presidents subject to the law, the coercive instance that safeguards the rights and obligations of the office. When this happens, it is because there is a translation of universal solidarity into the force of law that seeks to punish the holder of presidential power. However, what is common in democratic societies is that presidential power is constantly subjected to a normative framework of moral character and is questioned when it has deviated from its obligations and responsibilities. Through the communicative institution of public opinion, the presidential office is subjected to intense scrutiny with moral and symbolic consequences, often forcing the president to modify behavior or to directly confronts the accusations leveled against the individual holding office.

2.3   Presidential Office, Public Opinion, and Feminist Movements

We study the relationship among presidential office, public opinion, and feminist movements at the beginning of the 2020s, to illuminate how these three entities compete to attribute civil virtues and vices to each other in the face of women's demands to stop violence and femicide. We show how #MT, #NMCMV, and #UDSN managed to translate a series of behaviors attributed to the heteropatriarchal system and male sexual aggressiveness as anti-civil behavior. Such translations were attributed to presidential power and various social powers: men considered powerful, or institutions assumed as exclusionary. These movements also managed to translate demands for gender equality and respect for physical integrity as civil, thereby demanding civil reparation aimed at redressing and eliminating domination, discrimination and violence. This act of translation allowed women to move from being victims to being valued as heroes who tell their stories, resist, and fight to transform their environment. Therefore, we consider that the success of #MT, #NMCMV, and #UDSN was the result of their ability to translate violence and femicide into civil vices that must be curbed by public opinion and the state.

This translation was subjected to an alternative reading within the same discursive system. The president read the demands of feminist collectives as anti-civilian expressions: they were women who had a hidden agenda, who conspired against their government because they were manipulated by the dark powers of the opposition. Public opinion became a sounding board for the moral dispute between #MT, #NMCMV, and #UDSN and presidential power. Thus, arguments were wielded from the binary system of civil discourse in two directions. On the one hand, the idea was defended that feminist mobilizations were expressions of civil power, with presidential power detaching itself from its commitment as a universalist referent for the organization of authority and assuming anti-civil attributes. This scenario generated a growing demand, both from a part of the public and the feminist movement, for López Obrador to subject himself to the norms regarding the exercise of power granted to him by his office and to reestablish the duties and frameworks of action of the public function which, in normative terms, should exist on the side of civil power. On the other hand, there was support for the position that the feminist mobilizations were in fact actions underpinned by social powers that sought to delegitimize a president believed to embody the civil power of the country through the mandate he received at the ballot box, thereby representing progressive feminists. This positioning led certain members of the public to insist that the feminists mobilized against presidential power were not in fact *authentic* feminists.

As can be seen in Table 2.1, competing visions of public opinion over the meaning of feminist mobilizations were characterized by a relationship in which such mobilizations were considered civil if the presidential power was also considered civil (c, c). Conversely, mobilizations were considered anti-civil if presidential power was deemed civil (c, ac). If the mobilizations were evaluated as civil,

Table 2.1 Civil/anti-civil attribution system in public opinion
Source: Own elaboration

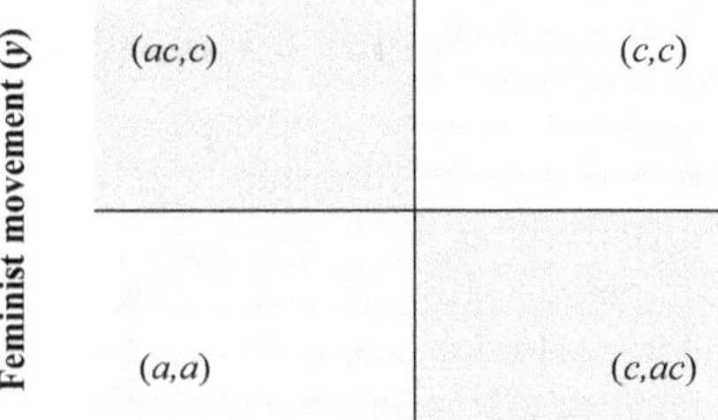

presidential power was interpreted as incapable of establishing a universal understanding of authority (*ac, c*). Finally, although both presidential power and feminist movements could potentially be interpreted as anti-civil, this was not evident in the analysis (*ac, ac*).

2.4 Methodology

The analytical reconstruction of the processes of tense intertwining and competition between presidential power and feminist movements through public opinion was conducted using a methodological strategy focused first on the reconstruction of a particular historical moment, namely, the rise of the first self-proclaimed leftist candidate and political party to the presidency of Mexico and the mobilization on a global scale of the #MeToo movement in the United States and France. In a second moment, we examined the periods of tension and conflict that emerged between presidential power (and its social power) and the civil power of the feminist movement. This conflict was identified through chronicles, opinions, criticisms and positionings in the media. In these discursive spaces, messages were constructed that translated the crisis situations through codes of the pure and impure by means of evaluations and narrative descriptions.

Media are a form of "situated knowledge," and they say much about how life and collectivities imagine themselves (Gupta, 2015). This perspective moves away from traditional and hegemonic views in the social sciences that examine media from a utilitarian model that assumes they are mere tools for political pressure. Such approaches (Salazar, 2022) reduce the analysis to vindicating or unmasking the progressive or conservative positions of the media, as well as the power networks behind them. A cultural sociological perspective recognizes that media and their journalists have diverse, sometimes hidden, intentions, but to translate them, journalists need a narrative that can only be drawn from historical cultural sedimentations. However, these narratives are subject to open interpretation, always open to be understood differently.

The opinions expressed in the media are not only ideological expressions and rhetorical resources of a strategic character; they are also statements that reveal efforts to signify the actions of #MT, #NMCMV and #UDSN to demand immediate action from the president to curb violence against women and femicide. We reviewed and analyzed these sets of discourses related to the disputes over #MT, #NMCMV and #UDSN. Our dataset included 233 notes and columns from *Reforma*—a liberal newspaper (Reyna et al., 2020), *La Jornada*—positioned to the left of the national political spectrum (Gutiérrez, 2015), *Milenio* and *El Universal*—considered at the center (Rodelo & Muñiz, 2017), and *Excélsior*—to the right of the political spectrum Lawson (2002). For each case analyzed, the information from the notes and news columns was collected and systematized, from the emergence of the event until the comments on the event disappeared and other events had captured the attention of public opinion.[4]

The newspapers reviewed were selected for several reasons: (1) each one presents in its content political news columns with different, sometimes even opposing, opinions; (2) they circulate digitally and in print at the national level; (3) they occupy a position within the traditional political spectrum ranging from the left to the right; and (4) they refer to each other both for critical purposes and to link comments. These relationships do not imply that they quote each other in a particular way but that their opinions and arguments are structured from defined patterns of social classification of the social and political actors to whom they refer. It is recognized that newspaper columns are biased in the interpretations they offer, because they start from interpretative frameworks anchored in different moral referents (Earl et al., 2004; McCarthy et al., 1996). This bias is important for the analysis because it allows us to understand how the interpretations activate, confront, and tensely intertwine different cultural codes. The news columns do not allow us to understand what "really" happened, even if they present evidence for or against certain actions and actors and show data of various kinds, but they do account for informed moral interpretations of an event.

Political news columns are important because they highlight public figures, moments of crisis, and alleged threats to social life. They allow the voices and speeches of the actors directly involved not to necessarily appear in the foreground, because precisely what is important is to show the competition among voices and to offer an interpretation. The goal is not so much to find the supposed "true meaning" of the speeches given by public figures in moments of crisis. The narrative constructions in the political news columns can provoke reactions of criticism or support for public figures and can sometimes alter the internal functioning of the institutions of the civil sphere. However, such judgments do not mean that political news columns necessarily produce social change or even influence public life. Their virtue lies in the fact that, as Butler and Luengo (2016) suggest, they construct messages through valuations and narratives that translate concrete situations into codes with apparent pretensions of truthfulness and universality. Such translations largely express the opinion shared and questioned by different groups on a broader scale.

To account for such translation, it is necessary to carry out an exploration that allows us to reconstruct the cultural structures and meanings within political news columns, to observe how they are connected in a broader and more coherent

---

[4] For the analysis, we used the universe of news columns published on the central issues of the period we studied. There was no sample selection, nor selection criteria to discriminate between one or the other: the total number of political news columns was reviewed as a whole body of data. For the analysis of #NMCMV, the universe of 68 newspaper columns was reviewed: *Excélsior* (8), *El Universal* (33), *Milenio* (8), *Reforma* (10) and *La Jornada* (9); for #UDSN, 125 columns where reviewed: *Excélsior* (23), *El Universal* (30), *Milenio* (25), *Reforma* (18) and *La Jornada* (29); and for #MT, 40 columns were reviewed: *Excélsior* (10), *El Universal* (11), *Milenio* (10), *Reforma* (5) and *La Jornada* (5). The decision to consider the universe of news columns aims at reconstructing and taking into account all opinions in order to show how they instantiate a set of deep cultural structures.

process. The commitment to a reading of this type implies carrying out "thick description," which allows us to unravel the structures of signification, and to determine their social field and their scope (Geertz, 2003). In media debates, it is possible to observe how the cultural forms that comprise public opinion, presidential power, and women's social mobilizations are articulated. These debates are understood as comments on something more than themselves; the origin of what is said, as Geertz (2003) himself warns, does not determine where it will be directed afterwards.

The debates analyzed in this book are symbolic acts that can be read as a social text (Ricoeur, 1984). Therefore, the objective is to analyze how the symbolic acts are interpreted and signified in repeated instantiations that respond to deep cultural structures. Instantiations in political news columns are not unique conjunctions, nor locally situated and unrepeatable meanings; they are expressions of collective representations anchored deep in a cultural structure.[5] In other words, "[T]hey are organized into narrative structures that locate actors and events in plots, assign moral responsibility, causality and agency, shape expectations of outcomes, and, in some cases, provide exemplary models for action" (Smith, 2005, p. 14).

To unravel this cultural structure, an ethnography of the narratives found in the political news columns was carried out. We accounted for how different social actors were assigned responsibility for an action or a reaction to what was seen as an effort to reduce or expand democratic spaces, to contaminate or purify a social mobilization, revealing the ways in which the columns opened, closed, or spliced with the presidential power or the mobilizations led by #MT, #NMCMV and #UDSN. Each column was interpreted based on the following series of questions. What motives were imputed to the president in carrying out his statements and positions on the #MT, #NMCMV, and #UDSN, and what motives were assigned to the movements? What relationships were attributed to presidential power, to López Obrador's allies with social power, and to the mobilizations of women under the #MT, #NMCMV and #UDSN banners? And, finally, to what kind of institutions did the president and #MT, #NMCMV, and #UDSN supposedly belong, and how did they forge ties (or not) with those who supported or criticized them for their positions?

With these questions, each news item was analyzed to discover the efforts made by different voices and social actors to control the meaning of certain events, especially those that sought to strengthen or transform the presidential figure and democratic institutions. These meanings form a framework of attributions in which different actors were pointed out as pure or impure, civil or anti-civil. Thus, the

---

[5] A limitation of this interpretation lies in the fact that the political news columns are only a way of instantiating the structures of cultural classification that exist in society. Anthropology also faces this problem. As Turner (2013) has shown, even in societies that are not highly differentiated, interpretations of the same ritual that has been put into practice since time immemorial have collectively shared meaning, but there are specific interpretations and variations. Following these coordinates, Augé (2010) argues that the media are anchored in deep classification structures that express differentiated positions that must be revealed in order to understand the moral sentiment of a society at a given time. News columns do not exhaust the totality of opinions of what happened; they are images that as a whole provide a portrait of what occurred, sometimes better than others.

methodological proposal developed in this book is not a semantic or structural analysis of the discourses, nor is it an analysis of opinion trends. It is an analysis that seeks to understand the deep cultural structures that underpin the discourses. This exercise in structural hermeneutics is composed of two moments.

The first of these moments refers to the effort that must be made to reconstruct texts as imbued with meaning, namely, textured networks of meanings through codes and narratives. The second moment refers to understanding how these texts are underpinned by signs and symbols defined in terms of patterned relationships with each other. Under these two premises, cultural sociology distances itself from hermeneutic efforts that understand culture as a simple text that is self-explanatory or that refers to culture in terms of abstract semantic logics. Structural hermeneutics makes it possible to understand culture as a factory of meaning that is sustained by a structure of deep cultural codes. Thus, it is possible to associate a set of meanings that emerge through events with historically sedimented deep cultural structures. In this way, every action, even if it is interpreted as instrumental, reflexive or constrained, is integrated in a horizon of meaning.

References

Alexander, J. (2006). *The civil sphere*. Oxford University Press.

Alexander, J. (2019). *What makes a social crisis? The problematization of social problems.* Polity Press.

Alexander, J., & Smith, P. (2003). *The strong program in cultural sociology: Elements of a structural hermeneutic*. Oxford University Press.

Augé, M. (2010). *Carnet de routes et de déroutes*. Galilée.

Butler, E., & Luengo, M. (2016). Conclusion: News innovation and enduring commitments. In J. Alexander, E. Butler, & M. Luengo (Eds.), *The crisis of journalism reconsidered* (pp. 282–290). Cambridge University Press.

Cardona, L., & Arteaga, N. (2020). "No me cuidan, me violan": The civil sphere and feminist protest. *Region and Society, 32*, e1345. https://doi.org/10.22198/rys2020/32/1345

Choi, J. (2019). South Korea's presidential scandal and civil repair. In J. Alexander, D. Palmer, S. Park, & A. Ku (Eds.), *The civil sphere in East Asia* (pp. 18–37). Cambridge University Press.

Dagnino, E., Olvera, A., & Panfichi, A. (2006). *La disputa por la construcción democrática en América Latina*. Fondo de Cultura Económica.

Earl, J., Martin, A., McCarthy, J., & Sarah, S. (2004). The use of newspaper data in the study of collective action. *Annual Review of Sociology, 30*, 65–80. https://doi.org/10.1146/annurev.soc.30.012703.110603

Eyerman, R., & Jamison, A. (1990). *Social movements: A cognitive approach*. Polity Press.

Geertz, C. (2003). *The interpretation of cultures*. Basic Books.

Gupta, A. (2015). Blurred boundaries: The discourse of corruption, the culture of politics, and the imagined state. In P. Abrams, A. Gupta, & T. Mitchell (Eds.), *Anthropology of the state* (pp. 71–144). Fondo de Cultura Económica.

Gutiérrez, A. E. (2015). Media, power, and violence in Nuevo León. In C. Del Palacio Montiel (Ed.), *Violence and regional journalism in Mexico* (pp. 255–288). National Council of Science and Technology.

Kivisto, P., & Sciortino, G. (2015). Introduction: Thinking the civil sphere. In P. Kivisto & G. Sciortino (Eds.), *Solidarity, justice and incorporation* (pp. 1–30). Oxford University Press.

Kivisto, P., & Sciortino, G. (2019). Conclusion: Reflections on radicalism and the civil sphere. In J. Alexander, T. Stack, & F. Khosrokhavar (Eds.), *Breaching the civil order: Radicalism and the civil sphere* (pp. 268–284). Cambridge University Press.

Lawson, H. (2002). *Building the fourth estate: Democratization and the rise of a free Press in Mexico*. University of California Press.

Lin, K. (2019). Developing communicative institutions in local communities: The practice of participatory budgeting in Taiwan. In J. Alexander, D. Palmer, S. Park, & A. Ku (Eds.), *The civil sphere in East Asia* (pp. 234–255). Cambridge University Press.

Luengo, M. (2018). Shaping solidarity in Argentina: The power of the civil sphere in repairing violence against women. In J. Alexander & C. Tognato (Eds.), *The civil sphere in Latin America* (pp. 39–65). Cambridge University Press.

Mast, J. (2006). The cultural pragmatics of event-ness: The Clinton / Lewinsky affair. In J. Alexander, B. Giesen, & J. Mast (Eds.), *Social performance: Symbolic action, cultural pragmatics, and ritual* (pp. 115–145). Cambridge University Press.

Mast, J. (2019). Introduction: Fragments, ruptures, and resurgent structures: The civil sphere and the fate of 'Civilship' in the Era of Trumpism. In J. Mast & J. Alexander (Eds.), *Politics of meaning/meaning of politics: Cultural sociology of the 2016 US presidential election* (pp. 1–16). Palgrave Macmillan.

McCarthy, J., McPhail, C., & Smith, J. (1996). Images of protest: Dimensions of selection bias in media coverage of Washington demonstrations, 1982 and 1991. *American Sociological Review, 61*(3), 478–499.

Reyna, V. H., Echeverría, M., & González, R. A. (2020). Beyond exogenous models: Mexican Journalism's modernization in its own terms. *Journalism Studies, 21*(13), 1815–1835. https://doi.org/10.1080/1461670X.2020.1796765

Ricoeur, P. (1984). The model of the text: Meaningful action considered as a text. *Social Research*, 185–218.

Rodelo, F., & Muñiz, C. (2017). Newspaper political orientation and its influence on the presence of framing and issues within the news. *Studies on the Journalistic Message, 23*(1), 241–256. https://doi.org/10.5209/ESMP.55594

Sachs, W., & Alexander, J. C. (2023). Presidential versus civil power: Public opinion, second-wave feminism, and party politics in the USA. *Cultural Sociology, 17*(1), 21–43.

Salazar, G. (2022). *Beyond violence. Alianzas y resistencia de la prensa local mexicana*. CIDE.

Shimizu, M. (2019). Institutions and civil instantiation: The case of modern Japanese police. In J. Alexander, D. Palmer, S. Park, & A. Ku (Eds.), *The civil sphere in East Asia* (pp. 188–212). Cambridge University Press.

Smith, P. (2005). *Why war? The cultural logic of Iraq, the Gulf War, and Suez*. University of Chicago Press.

Thumala, M. (2018). Civil indignation in Chile: Recent collusion scandals in the retail industry. In J. Alexander, D. Palmer, S. Park, & A. Ku (Eds.), *The civil sphere in East Asia* (pp. 66–92). Cambridge University Press.

Tognato, C. (2021). Commentary: Demarcating constructive from destructive populisms: Civil translation vs. civil mimicry. In J. Alexander, G. Sciortino, & P. Kivisto (Eds.), *Populism in the civil sphere* (pp. 278–286). Polity Press.

Turner, V. (2013). *La selva de los símbolos*. Siglo XXI.

Villegas, C. (2019). The middle class as a culture structure: Rethinking middle-class formation and democracy through the civil sphere. *American Journal of Cultural Sociology, 7*(2), 135–173.

Weber, M. (1979). *Economía y Sociedad*. Fondo de Cultura Económica.

Chapter 3
#MeToo and *Autre Parole*: The Global Problem of Harassment

Abstract This chapter examines the public debate on a global scale around the confrontation between *#Metoo* and *Autre Parole*. Both movements positioned themselves differently with regard to the demands for sanction, redress, and reparations in the face of cases of harassment and violence against women, particularly within the artistic world. This debate was characterized by two competing discourses that sought to legitimize and contaminate the claims and demands. The discourses of public opinion—as a symbolic representation that crystallizes the "public"—typified positions as morally justified or not, based on the social and historical attributions made to the representatives of *#Metoo* and *Autre Parole*, the way in which they evaluated the liberating and oppressive capacities of sexuality, and the way in which they defined situations of harassment or seduction.

Keywords Global civil sphere · Feminist mobilization · Violence against women · Harassment · #MeToo · Autre parole

3.1 *#MeToo* and Civil Repair

African American activist Tarana Burke was the first woman to use the phrase *Metoo* ("Me too") on the now defunct social network *Myspace* around 2006. Her aim was to generate empathy among African American women from marginalized areas of the United States who had been victims of sexual abuse. From her perspective, such empathy would encourage the empowerment of black women living in impoverished spaces. According to Burke, the phrase was inspired by the reflection she made after remaining silent in the face of an account of a sexual assault shared

L. A. Cardona Acuña, N. Arteaga Botello, *Feminism, Power and Public Opinion in Mexico*, SpringerBriefs in Sociology,
https://doi.org/10.1007/978-3-032-14141-5_3

with her by a thirteen-year-old girl.[1] The phrase became popular globally in October, 2017, when actor Alyssa Milano used it to denounce the sexual harassment she had suffered at the hands of film producer Harvey Weinstein. "If every woman who has been sexually harassed or assaulted," Milano warned, "would tweet the words *MeToo* we could show people the magnitude of the problem."[2] While her proposal to use the hashtag *#MeToo* was not directly related to the movement Burke originally spearheaded, Milano acknowledged on Twitter that it was significant that the two stories were connected.[3]

According to social media reports, on October 16, 2017 alone, the phrase *#MeToo* was tweeted more than half a million times, while on Facebook, it was posted on the platform by more than 4.7 million people in 12 million posts in a period of 24 hours.[4] In addition to the massive reach of the hashtag, several actors joined Milano's campaign, among them, Patricia Arquette, Björk, Sherl Crow, Viola Davis, Lady Gaga, Monica Lewinsky, Uma Thurman, Lane Moore, and Reese Witherspoon. Denouncements from the artistic milieu were joined by others in academia[5] and politics.[6] A month later, the "Survivors of *#MeToo*" march was organized in the streets of Hollywood.

The movement born in the United States soon transcended its borders. In a period of about 2 months, hundreds of opinion columns, reports, and interviews on radio and television precipitated a discussion in countries around the world. At the same time, waves of harassment reports emerged, with different impacts. In one case, opinion columns reflected how the actions of both U.S. and French female actors were interpreted by different audiences. In another, harassment complaints reverberated throughout Western European countries, including Iceland, Sweden, China, India, Africa, Latin America, and Great Britain.[7] Allegations were made on social networks following the *#MeToo* strategy. The response also included censorship of *hashtags* related to *#MeToo*, as in the Chinese case, where it was considered "a destabilizing movement coming from abroad," and the proposal of laws to combat harassment in some Western European countries.[8]

In the midst of this global reaction, a group of 300 female actors organized the *Times Up* collective, in which Ashley Judo, Eva Longoria, America Ferrara, Natalie Portman, and Emma Stone, among others, participated.[9] The collective sought not only to denounce sexual harassment in the world of Hollywood show business, but also in other sectors of society that, due to economic and social conditions, did not

---

[1] The Boston Globe (2017, October 17).

[2] D'Zurilla (2017, October 16).

[3] Ohlheiser (2017, October 19).

[4] Ibid.

[5] Neill (2017).

[6] Cadei (2017, October 25).

[7] Associate Press (AP) (2018).

[8] Ibid.

[9] Faus (2018, January 1).

have the possibility of making their experiences visible. At the Golden Globe Awards, on January 7, 2018, *Times Up* proposed that attendees dress in black, as a sign of protest against sexual harassment.

During the ceremony, African American actor and journalist Opera Winfrey gave a speech in which she warned of the need to stop harassment and denounce harassers. For Oprah, the victims were many: "domestic workers, rural workers, chefs, scientists, doctors, engineers in the technology industry and the military, in politics and business," They now live "under a culture broken by powerful men. For too long women were not heard when they spoke truth to power from those men. But their time is over. Their time is over. Their time is over."[10] Thus, Oprah warned:

> I want to tell all those girls watching TV from home that a new day is coming. And when that new day begins it will be because thousands of women, many of them here, and some phenomenal men, brought us a little closer to the time when no one has to say 'Me too' anymore.[11]

The impact of this speech—broadcast on a global scale—had an enormous effect on public opinion in different countries. It immediately connected with movements such as the French *BalanceTonPorc* ("Denounce your pig"), the *#QuellaVoltaChe* ("That time when") in Italy and generated replicas in the Hispanic world with *#YoTambién* in Spain and Latin America. However, Oprah's speech, which somehow crystallized the ideology of the *Time's Up* and the *#MeToo* collectives, was not without its critics. Tanara Burke, who had forged the *MeToo* phrase, pointed out that the U.S. female actors' movement left the work of African American women from marginalized areas in oblivion, work that not only sought denunciation, but also dialogue about the meaning of sexual aggression suffered by women. Although Burke criticized the Hollywood female actors' movement, she nevertheless acknowledged the work they were doing. On the other side of the Atlantic, in France, a movement critical of *MeToo* sparked a debate on a broader scale, also led by a group of female actors and artists, most of them of French origin.[12]

The collective of 100 women led by, among others, film icon Catherine Deneuve, writer Catherine Millet, and singer Ingrid Caven, published an open letter in the newspaper *Le Monde* entitled *Une autre parole: Des femmes libèrent une autre parole* ("Another word: Women launch another word"), on January 9, 2 days after the awards ceremony. In this document, she acknowledged that the Weinstein case had triggered "a legitimate awareness of sexual violence against women in the professional sphere, where certain men abuse their power. This is necessary. However, they warned that this position had now been transformed into its opposite". According to the open letter, we are ordered to speak out, to silence what angers, and if there is anyone who refuses to comply with these orders, they are accused of being traitors, accomplices of male power. The letter's subscribers warned that this is characteristic of puritanism,

---

[10] Russonello (2018, January, 6).

[11] Ibid.

[12] Hill (2017, October 16).

> to borrow, in the name of a pretended general good, the arguments of the protection of women and their emancipation in order to chain them to a status of eternal victims, of poor little things under the influence of phallocrat demons, as in the good old days of witchcraft.

In this way, the authors of the open letter accused the *#Metoo* movement of carrying out a campaign of denunciation and public accusation of people who had no possibility of responding or defending themselves, putting them on the same level as sexual aggressors. This scenario generated—according to the authors—an expeditious justice that immediately generates its victims: men sanctioned in the exercise of their profession, who are forced to resign because they made a mistake "by touching a knee, trying to steal a kiss, talking about intimate things at a business dinner, or sending sexually explicit messages" to a woman who was not attracted to them. According to the signatories, this need to send *pigs* to the slaughter—in reference to the *BalanceTonPorc* movement—did not help women to empower themselves but rather served the interests of the "enemies of sexual freedom," "religious extremists," the worst "reactionaries" who consider the need to guarantee a substantial conception of good and Victorian morality, that women are "beings apart," "girls with adult faces" who demand to be protected at all times. In this sense, the letter accused movements such as *#Metoo* or *BalanceTonPorc* of calling upon men to search in their most distant past and in their deepest conscience, those times when they had acted out of place and for which they must repent publicly. It represented a demand for a public confession, according to these French female actors, by the self–proclaimed *#Metoo* prosecutors, which instilled the "climate of a totalitarian society."

The letter, signed by the French female actors and artists, warned that what they called "the purifying wave" no longer recognized any limits. It was being demanded, according to them, that works of art—such as those of Schiele or Balthus—be censored because they represented an apology for pedophilia. It was also demanded that a retrospective of Roman Polanski, accused of raping a U.S. underaged actor in the 1960s, be banned, and that exhibitions of filmmaker Jean-Claude Brisseau, accused of promising to include three women in one of his films in exchange for filming them having sex, be postponed. Finally, there were accusations regarding publishers demanding from essayists and novelists that their male characters be portrayed as less "sexist" and that female traumas be portrayed in a more obvious and sometimes exaggerated manner.

Taking Ruwen Ogien's proposal as a point of reference, namely, that there must be freedom of offense for artistic freedom, the position of the group of French women who sent the letter to *Le Monde* considered that the freedom to importune should be defended, since it is indispensable to sexual freedom. They believed that women today are sufficiently warned that the sexual drive is by nature offensive and savage, but they are also intelligent enough not to mistake a clumsy flirtation for a sexual attack. Moreover, a person is not a monolithic entity:

> [A] woman can, in the same day, manage a professional team and be the sexual object of a man, without being a 'whore' or a vile accomplice of the patriarchy. She can see that her salary is equal to a man's but not be forever traumatized by a groper on the subway, even if that is considered a crime. She can see this as the expression of great sexual misery, as a non-event.

The letter ended by pointing out that they do not identify with that feminism which, beyond denouncing abuses of power, takes on the face of hatred towards men. They assured that the freedom to say no to a sexual proposition is not possible without the freedom to intrude. The way to respond to this freedom to intrude did not involve pigeonholing women forever in the role of prisoner and victim. It was necessary to teach girls, as they pointed out, to be aware, so that they do not allow themselves to be intimidated, but also so that they do not allow themselves to be blamed. They must be educated by warning them that incidents that affect their bodies as women do not necessarily compromise their dignity and they must not turn these incidents into a mechanism that transforms them into the "perpetual victim." Women are not—stated those who signed the letter published in *Le Monde*—reducible to their bodies.

The diffusion of *#Metoo* and *Autre Parole* triggered a dispute based on the binary coding system of civil discourse. Both movements were qualified as civil and anti-civil within public opinion, as a structure of feelings in democratic life. In the news columns on the subject, social class (poor/rich), race (white/non-white), temporality in activism (old/new feminist), moral position (puritan/libertarian), seriousness of aggression (seduction/harassment), and centrality of the feminine (spirit/body) were identified as referents of purification, as civil virtues, and contamination, namely, anti-civil characteristics. The competing discourses defined a symbolic dispute in relation to civil redress for acts of violence and sexual harassment towards women, as well as differentiated interpretations of their rights, equality and gender equity.[13]

3.2   The Anti-Civil Nature of *Autre Parole*

Within public opinion, *Autre Parole* was characterized as an expression with all the contaminating attributes of civil discourse. It was seen as a front opened with the aim of fracturing the feminist movement and pitting women against each other, that is, breaking the logics of solidarity and inclusion among women. The movement

---

[13] The construction of the debate was analyzed within communicative institutions, particularly in the press of certain Ibero-American countries (Argentina, Colombia, Ecuador, Spain, Mexico and Peru), France, the United States and England. We reviewed 475 columns published between January 9 and March 27, 2018, a period in which the debate was active in news media. The search keywords we used included the names of the two movements, for searches in Google, Google Scholar, Proquest, and the most widely circulated newspapers in the countries analyzed. Each of the journalistic references was analyzed by locating what kind of motives, relationships and institutions were imputed to both *#Metoo* and *Autre Parole*. First, a record was taken of whether each position was considered a rational, reasonable, realistic, and objective expression—an act of agency—or on the contrary, irrational, prejudiced, unrealistic and subjective - an act subjected to the normative structures of domination. Second, a record was taken of whether each position was evaluated as the expression of women in open, critical, and frank relationships, that is, full of civil virtues, or closed, discretionary, and oriented to benefit a sector of the population, e.g., men or women. Third, the type of institutions they supposedly defended was recorded: regulated, under the rule of law, equitable, and inclusive or, on the contrary, arbitrary, discretionary, hierarchical, and exclusionary.

was accused of embodying selfish motives, oriented to benefit men and their structures of domination. It was also assumed that *Autre Parole* had a profound ignorance of the real conditions among women and therefore came from women of privileged upper social classes, most likely white, who ignored the obstacles faced by lower-class women and women of color. Likewise, it was assumed that the relationships sustained by *Autre Parole* were closed, emblematic of its dominant and hegemonic class and racial status. Furthermore, it was charged that *Autre Parole* sought to sustain social hierarchies by concealing the conditions of submission and domination (hierarchies considered anti-civil) that govern the relations between men and women, thus guaranteeing the reproduction of the patriarchal culture. Finally, it was judged that their attitude eroded the role of the institutions in charge of curbing violence against women, especially when *Autre Parole* insisted that women should reflect on whether they were really facing a situation of harassment or a clumsy act of gallantry.

The French manifesto was interpreted as an expression by women unable to understand the changes in the codes that govern relationships between men and women. As pointed out by Dubois (cited by Peker, 2018), the French intellectuals, businesswomen and journalists who signed the manifesto stopped their intelligence in order not to step into a courtroom, where they did not know how to play, an unknown terrain where they would have to reinvent the codes that gave foundation to their successful lives. It was ostensibly a Western and white manifesto (Adler, in Lehoux, 2018), which minimized the situation of women globally (Beltran, 2018; Latapí, 2018; Collado, 2018; Dunham, 2017). According to Kislinger (2018), it was the product of resentment and confusion, if one takes into consideration that harassment is still considered by many as "natural" in society.

Second, it was highlighted that the signatories to the letter came from favored groups. It was the discourse of women living in a privileged social context who defended "the right to importune," minimizing the experiences of those who have lived through harassment (Collado, 2018) and the cultural rupture introduced by *#Metoo* (Gersen, 2017). The manifesto expressed the "counter-revolution of the privileged against the disenfranchised" (Merino, 2018; Olavarría, 2018). As suggested by a group of feminists led by Caroline de Haas, *Autre Parole* denounced macho sexism when it emanated from men in popular neighborhoods, "but leave the hand up the ass" of those men when they are from the same social milieu. The critics of *Autre Parole* suggested that this strange ambivalence made it possible to appreciate the feminism they were defending (France Télévisions, 2018). According to Lamas (2018), the central flaw of *Autre Parole* manifested in not knowing the difference when denouncing the harassment of a European or North American female actor from that targeting a worker, a domestic employee, a peasant, an office worker, or a secretary.

Critics warned of the classist character of the manifesto, which had no place when it comes to respecting the dignity of women (Amo, 2018; Europa Press, 2018; De Hass, cited in Mascia, 2018; Thomas, 2018). Those who subscribed to *Autre Parole* were women who are "deaf, blind, living in a 'Paris-white-between-the-walls'" (Priego-Broca, 2018). This status prevented them from seeing beyond their noses, as De Anda (in Lucario, 2018f), and they were oblivious to recognize the privilege of not taking a touch or a sexual innuendo badly. In this sense, *Autre Parole* was considered the reflection of the trivialization and emptying of meanings about what feminism is (García, 2018). This opinion was also shared by Dresser (2018) and Bernal-Triviño (2018), who described the manifesto as a "trivial act," of insensitive, reductionist language, in which its authors seemed to be willing to forgive everything.

Third, the manifesto was described as ambivalent, defending the right to importune in sexual matters (Cruz, 2018). For some analysts, the French women, led by Deneuve and Millet, assumed that all women could simply say "no" to a sexual innuendo, without considering their socioeconomic or cultural characteristics (Torreblanca et al., 2018). The positioning of the French women was also labeled as "terrifying," by supporting the naturalization of a practice through which many women had been victims (Díaz, 2018; Revuelta, 2018). In addition, it was a response from the "pigs and their allies who have reason to worry because things are changing for them" (France Télévisions, 2018).

According to Wiener (2018a), "[T]he manifesto is a revenge of patriarchy, written by women who act as accomplices of a perverse system." García (2018) agreed, stating that it was a strategy against the advancement of young women rebelling against injustice and allying themselves with feminism. As suggested by De Haas (in Mascia, 2018) and Munker (2018), for the "pigs and their allies, the old world is on its way to disappear, very slowly, but inexorably (France Télévisions, 2018).

In some news columns, it was judged that the French women only sought to draw attention to the female actors behind *#Metoo* (Europa Press, 2018). Their statements were described as "dissonant voices" in the face of the advances in equality sought by *#Metoo* (Dumitru, in La Voz de Galicia, 2018). For Luciana Peker (2018), the document had an impact and hurt because it came from women who surely suffered some kind of harassment. The manifesto was described as "absurd writing," considering what feminism against sexual harassment intends. The female actors who signed it were wrong, according to their critics, because they pit women against other women. According to Ares (in Europa Press, 2018) and Sánchez-Mellado (2018), the publication of French women was inconvenient, coming at a time when things can definitely change. In this sense, it was unfortunate how and when it was published (Lamas, 2018; Solórzano in Lucario, 2018b; Peker, 2018). Finally, some critics pointed out that the position of *Autre Parole* should have been understood from the social and intellectual history of France, in which the mechanisms of opportunity for women were constantly cancelled (García 2018). It should not be surprising, for example, that the manifesto represented "a coup that comes from a France that was the cradle of feminism, but that post-1789 denied political rights to women."

The anti-civil motives attributed to *Autre Parole* within public opinion had their correlate in the imputation made to the relations between men and women. It was pointed out, first of all, that *Autre Parole* did not consider the fact that men take advantage of their positions of power to harass (West, 2018); in other words, power asymmetries in sex/gender relations were neglected (Lamas, 2018; De Anda in Lucario, 2018f; Europa

Press, 2018). This is why *Autre Parole* ended up justifying the actions of predators (Félix, 2018; Gérard, 2018). As Réjane Sénac (2018) and Casanova (2018) suggest, the manifesto ignored that so-called "seduction à la française" conceals the asymmetry between the sexes and, for some reason, its disappearance unsettles them (Belaich, 2018). In France, the relations between men and women, stated Catherie Achin (in Raulin et al., 2018), were constituted based not on equality, but on discrimination of the sexes (Belaich, 2018). If the French are seductive, it is always in the masculine form, not in the feminine (Montreynaud, cited in Belaich, 2018).

Second, it was asserted that *Autre Parole* overlooked female-male relationships in workspaces, where "a *lie-down*, groping or outings" with the boss are commonplace (Lamas, 2018; Carlson & Carlson, 2017). The French women's mistake was to include the idea of sexual freedom in the work context (Dumitru in La Voz de Galicia, 2018). By saying that harassment should not be confused with clumsy behavior, the French women took, according to Salvador (2018), a maternal attitude towards men that justified their action against women who play "lady and gentleman" but do not yet know how to do it. The defense of men, as Peker (2018) warned, was unnecessary, since they do not need female defenders. Gallic female actors, noted De Anda (in Lucario, 2018f) "do not see the difference between the places of seduction and the person who is intended with equal or no conditions, that makes a difference regarding the consequences when refusing."

According to Lamas (2018) and Hubbard (2017), *Autre Parole* elided the structural violence behind relationships between men and women. In the same sense, Salas (in Lucario, 2018c) pointed out that when we speak of stalking or harassment, we speak of the exercise of power, of domination. When an aggressor objectifies a woman, abuses her position, this action cannot be interpreted as part of men's sexual freedom. Harassment is a tool that men use to condition women's access to the labor and economic world. *Autre Parole* drew a blurred line between seduction and harassment, warned Amo (2018) and Stephens (2017), damaging the credibility of women who report it. By not separating harassment and freedom, French women vindicated macho power over women's bodies and erotic will (Cacho, in Mural de Negro, 2018; Berrin, 2017).

Although the *Autre Parole* manifesto suggested that any bodily aggression should not undermine the spiritual integrity of women, it could not be ignored, as Adler (in Lehoux, 2018) and Collins (2018) pointed out, that any attack on the body translates immediately and consubstantially into physical aggression. When a woman is assaulted, it is because she is considered an object (Lehoux, 2018). As Lévy-Willard (2018) pointed out, the women behind *Autre Parole* ignored that anthropologists explain that women's bodily control has the function of guaranteeing their servitude in human societies. In conclusion, the *Autre Parole* position is not able to distinguish seduction and gallantry from harassment and violence against women (De Anda, in Lucario, 2018f), reproducing the traditional ideas that exist about love and sex (Ruiz, 2018). We should question ourselves, suggested De Anda (in Lucario, 2018f) and Wiener (2018b), about how *Autre Parole* came to propose to us that it is necessary to defend harassing men and blame women who have been harassed.

Critics of the manifesto considered that the trivialization of harassment as "clumsy flirting" hindered the operation of institutions that address and sanction violence against women. Their position required women to value their experience as unimportant or less serious than other rights violations (Coll, 2018, Filipovic, 2017). For detractors of the French text, the *Autre Parole* represented a defense of what men want: "to perpetuate and overlap a macho culture where inequality is present" (Díaz, 2018). Other critics suggested that *Autre Parole* "proposed women endure harassment when it should reflect on new ways of relating to each other romantically and sexually" (Torreblanca et al., 2018). For Ruiz (2018), for example, the denunciation "breaks an alliance with men that has been comfortable for women who say that to point out harassment is to exaggerate and so they receive validation from the males around them."

For Faur (2018), French women were denying harassment and adding arguments to one of the contemporary gender myths: harassment is an invention to "fuck" men. Thus, *Autre Parole* ended up defending the freedom of "any Harvey Weinstein" in the world. It similarly concealed, as Adler noted (in Lehoux, 2018), the fact that there exists in the West male domination that is exercised politically, legally, sexually and intellectually. The French signatories were accused of betraying "the daily battle of thousands of women in the world against sexual harassment." In fact, Priego-Broca (2018), Solórzano (in Lucario, 2018b) and De la Peña (2018) stated that "declaring themselves 'in response to' was very unfortunate" especially as opposed to *#Metoo*. Moreover, the manifesto failed to caricature Anglo-Saxon puritanism as the main enemy to be defeated in at least two ways. First, they decontextualized North American puritanism (Cacho, in Mural de Negro, 2018; Melgar, 2018), and second, as Carmen Boullosa warned in an interview with Sandra Lucario (2018a), they failed to provide "an alternative point of view on the bifocal intolerances of Anglo-Saxon puritanism".

According to Salas (in Lucario, 2018c), an important sector of feminists dissociated themselves from the French manifesto, because they qualified it as a declaration of war against feminism and therefore, it did not represent them (Borrelli, cited by Peker, 2018). *Autre Parole* was championed by "women who are repeat offenders when it comes to pedophile advocacy and rape apologists, [who use] their media visibility to trivialize sexual violence [and] disregard the fact that millions of women suffer or have suffered this type of violence" (Wiener, 2018a). The *Autre Parole* was labeled an "antifeminist" text by Regina Tamés (in Lucario, 2018e) and Cárdenas (in Wiener, 2018a), because it pointed out that harassment is a "confusing" thing, instead of drawing attention to the fundamental debate on consent. However, for other French activists (Adler, in Lehoux, 2018), the French text fractured solidarity among women by introducing the idea that some confuse harassment with gallantry.

3.3   The Civil Nature of Autre Parole

The public discourses that supported *Autre Parole* claimed that it was a manifesto motivated by the defense of freedom and the sexual drive of women and men—principles that were part of French history and culture—and that underpinned individual liberty. According to the arguments of those in favor of *Autre Parole*, the text invited the recognition of women as full-fledged erotic agents and not as infants in a permanent state of victimization. To the extent that this was recognized, it would be possible to guarantee the construction of equitable relations with men. Finally, it was noted that *Autre Parole* demanded the opening of a debate on harassment that would have an impact on institutional designs, to account for the spatial-temporal circumstances in which it occurred, with the aim of clarifying misunderstandings, thereby ensuring justice and due process for both victims and alleged harassers.

Those who supported *Autre Parole* pointed out that the manifesto was motivated by the defense of sexual freedom (Tamés, in Lucario, 2018e; Faur, 2018; Fernández, 2018), and by a claim, according to Andión (in Lucario, 2018g), not to condemn any sexuality. The French positioning worked to integrate into the debate the issue of consent from an intersectional perspective (Torreblanca et al., 2018; Ruiz, 2018). It was a direct positioning without prudery, healthy and courageous (González, 2018; Barbier, in Mascia, 2018). It was a document that broke down the wall of political correctness, giving voice to feminists who thought differently about harassment (Sastre, in Gérard, 2018; Rodríguez, 2018; Díaz, 2018). It broke with single or condescending discourses (Ferreyra, 2018; Morejón, 2018). According to Viennot (2018) the text was a provocative, well-argued, and intellectually elaborated action, indeed, a position against Ortho-feminism, a unique and hegemonic type of feminism that closes the door to other feminisms. The text supposedly aimed at reflection and not at "witch-hunting" (De Paz, 2018; Mascia, 2018). Those who subscribed to *Autre Parole* were judged in civil terms: they were women "courageous and provocative [who] denounce a climate of totalitarian society" (Nebot, 2018) and who revealed the "fucked-up rules" that some female actors have taken advantage of to make a career (Lamas, 2018).

According to Ayuso (2018), Cacho (in Mural de Negro, 2018), and Tagle (in Lucario, 2018d), the French women's position claimed that sexuality is delicious and incites play, without being invasive or unequal. *Autre Parole* recalled that censorship and morality place restrictions and normalize the relationship between men and women (Zárate, 2018). This positioning, as Ferreyra (2018), Marco, (2018), and Faur (2018) warned, was not all violence; there is desire, love, friendship and pleasure that cannot be subjected to regulatory mechanisms to be safe from any misunderstanding. Sexuality is made up of encounters, disagreements, hits and misses, so flirting or seduction should not be repressed (Dumitru, in La Voz de Galicia, 2018).

Seduction, noted Podirier (2018), "is an innocuous and pleasant game, dating back to the times of medieval 'courtly love' [...] that is why there has always been a kind of harmony between the sexes that is particularly French." La *Autre Parole* defended the right to surprise and be surprised (Salvador, 2018; Nebot 2018). As Anne Morelli (in, RTBF, 2018) asserted, #*Metoo* left out the fact that women also seduce, flirt and harass, so they are not always victims (Razer, 2018; Weiss, 2018; RTBF, 2018). Feminist Valérie Toranian (2018) pointed out that the problem was not in sex, but in power: power is what creates abuse, not sex. There is always a serial seducer next to the man of power, just as there are women with power who are serial seducers.

Public opinion that supported *Autre Parole* highlighted sexual freedom and freedom of thought, relativizing the significance of the body in women's lives. French women defended what happens to the body but did not accord it so much importance, inviting us to rethink how much we yield the excessive valuation of the body in our lives to patriarchy (Nebot 2018; Ferreyra 2018, Morelli, in RTBF, 2018). This belief does not imply that what a man does with a woman's body is not serious, according to Viennot (2018) and Sastre (in Gérard, 2018), but it cannot mark women's lives.

According to Marco (2018) and Viennot (2018), *Autre Parole* did not defend harassers or machismo, but warned that rapists and those men who grope in the subway or on the street are not the same. *Autre Parole* pointed out that one cannot equate the actions of Hollywood producers and harassment in public transportation, because then harassment becomes a catch-all for the many forms suffering experienced by women. The positioning of French women was considered the expression of intellectuals with a sexual life that does not fit an agenda, women capable of accepting a vibrator as an anniversary present (Salvador, 2018). Thus, *Autre Parole* was valued as the expression of women with rational and autonomous (civil) motives.

Autre Parole was also interpreted based on the type of relationships it suggested. To understand its context, it is necessary to consider the historical, social, and intellectual sedimentations of France. The manifesto was associated with claims dating back to the eighteenth century: "[S]ome of the icons are the discussion salons, various concepts of sexual freedom. Feminism could not be conceived without their contributions. Her manifesto is not to be missed" (González, 2018). Those who supported the *Autre Parole* saw in French feminists—as Salvador (2018) did—the vanguard of sexual liberation in the twentieth century, which embodied expressions ranging from orgies to sadomasochistic practices or experimentation, as well as any kind of sexual daring.

For some commentators, *Autre Parole* feminism highlighted difference: the possibility of a sexuality outside the patriarchal gaze (Martínez, 2018; Cruz, 2018). Proponents of the manifesto suggested that French women do not recognize themselves in man-hating feminism (Podirier, 2018). They rejected puritanism because French literature and culture are characterized by libertinism, gallantry, and sexual freedom crystallized in the Marquis de Sade, Michel Foucault, or Choderlos de Laclos (Mascia, 2018; Dudda, 2018). The manifesto was seen by its advocates as reflecting a more permissive culture that understands sexuality as an integral part of life (Estremadoiro, 2018).

Some commentators, as de facto representatives of civil society discourse, linked *Autre Parole* to De Beauvoir's thinking. De Beauvoir warned that American women and men act as if they do not like each other, incapable of generating bonds of friendship. Between them there is distrust, and they relate to each other through petty grievances and disputes (Podirier, 2018). Not all women, Tamés (in Lucario, 2018e) and Morejón (2018) asserted, are victims, nor are all men aggressors. Women cannot be condemned to their permanent infantilization (Podirier, 2018; Solórzano, in Lucario, 2018b; Nebot, 2018; Atwood, 2018). If women possess agency, seduction is a two-way relationship, a voluntary dance between two (Cacho, in Mural de Negro, 2018; Atwood, 2018). For some commentators, such as Ferreyra (2018), the French women who signed the letter invited us to think about whether it is true that men manage and impose their desire on women.

For the supporters of *Autre Parole*, seduction vindicated the male erotic drive. It is not by condemning male desire but by sharing it with women that they would achieve emancipation (Mascia, 2018). The female actors behind the French manifesto had given voice to men in the face of silence or acceptance without defense by those who accused them. In other words, men do not go around the world harassing women (Lozada, 2018; Ferreyra, 2018), even though, as Lamas (2018) and Merkin (2018) pointed out, "women use their erotic capital to get things and most likely men misinterpret those messages."

The vindication of the masculine suggests that overcoming patriarchy cannot be achieved by lynching men, renouncing the conquests of body and sex, annulling works of art as catharsis, committing creative freedom to the most reactionary censorships (Morejón, 2018; De la Barreda, 2018). *Autre Parole* encouraged men and women to make things happen, sexually speaking, without justifying violence, but betting on empowered, improvised, and spontaneous women (Ferreyra, 2018; Faur, 2018). The manifesto was interpreted as a call to curb puritan hysteria in the name of women's dignity (see for example, De la Peña, 2018; Rodríguez, 2018; Díaz, 2018; González, 2018; Torreblanca et al., 2018). Consequently, it was labeled as "resistance to puritan feminism" (Mascia, 2018; Tamés, in Lucario, 2018e; Andión, in Lucario, 2018g; Martínez, 2018; Dumitru, in La Voz de Galicia, 2018; Andrade, 2018).

In terms of the institutions that *Autre Parole* sought to build, they would be in charge of justice that would put the presumption of innocence and due process for alleged harassers first (Tamés, in Lucario, 2018e; Atwood, 2018). The *#Metoo* social media denunciation strategy was qualified as being excessive. Being accused of harassment implies being judged as guilty (Merkin, 2018). *Autre Parole* was a call to stop "thought police" and a McCarthyist policy of persecution (Podirier, 2018; Gill, 2018). French women bring the debate to the intimate, away from the public (Méndez, 2018), which accommodated a variety of circumstances that can hardly be judicialized. De Paz (2018) added that it is necessary to curb the pointing of blame at men for something they have not done, or something that could have been misinterpreted. *Autre Parole* suggested instead an open debate to help understand the dimensions of harassment.

Supporters of *Autre Parole* noted that the debate was enriched by bringing various points of view to the table and nuancing the issue of harassment. An interesting discussion was opened, according to Lucario (2018e), Méndez (2018), De Paz (2018), and Nebot (2018), about sexual relations. Although it was admittedly published at the wrong time, it stimulated frank conversations that favor broadly discussing harassment without preconceptions and prejudices (Tamés, in Lucario, 2018e; Díaz, 2018). Those who supported the manifesto noted that its greatest achievement was to discuss "what is considered a sex crime, where is the border between seduction and sexual aggression?" (García, 2018; Madrid, 2018), a space in which confusion reigns, difficult to regulate (Viennot, 2018), but which should help differentiate between flirting and rape (Andrade, 2018). As Sastre posited (in Gérard, 2018), U.S. female actors put forward a different argument: women are little red riding hoods ready to be devoured by the wolf, without wondering about their complicity in putting their sexuality as a bargaining chip to obtain a film role.

3.4 Two Forms of Civil Repair

The dispute generated within public opinion around *#Metoo* and *Autre Parole* on harassment, was defined by two competing discourses that, despite their differences, adhered to the codes and meanings of civil discourse. As Kivisto and Sciortino (2015) have suggested, conflicts over resources and mechanisms of ascription and exclusion are conflicts over their interpretation. Competing positions stated that harassment should be reported, women should be subject to civil redress and perpetrators punished. However, they differed on the meaning of harassment, how it should be reported, and the role of institutions. The difference was constructed on the basis of the imputations wielded by the comments for and against *#Metoo* and *Autre Parole*. These imputations were structured through a set of binary codes in which the pure and impure, or civil or anti-civil, character of both positions was pointed out.

The negative class imputations against *Autre Parole* first considered their voice invalid because it represented the white French bourgeoisie, closed in on itself, ignorant of the lives of other women.[14] Second, they were accused being a voice from another era, in which sexual freedom was considered a means to equality, ignoring the fact that this did not upset gender asymmetries. The defenders of *Autre Parole* argued against *#Metoo* and its puritanical spirit that generated mechanisms of social and moral control, very much in tune with the spirit of conservatives.

Autre Parole was seen as moving away from religion to revitalize the history of French sexual liberalism that dated to the eighteenth century. The voices in favor of French female actors endorsed the commitment to freedom, sexual drives, and erotic agency in both sexes. All these elements were constitutive of the "natural" character of gender relations. These positions reflected the idea that where there is seduction and flirtation there will be confusion. However, the supposedly liberating character of *Autre Parole* was interpreted by *#Metoo* advocates as a defense of patriarchal structures that prevent seduction and flirtation from being free, egalitarian and equitable. The dispute over the meaning of seduction and harassment

---

[14] The #Metoo movement was also accused of having a class bias by Tarana Burke, who in 2006 launched the phrase *Metoo* on MySpace to generate empathy among African-American women from marginalized areas of the United States who had been victims of sexual abuse. Burke noted that the U.S. female actors' movement neglected the work of African-American women, who sought not only to denounce but to dialogue about the meaning of sexual assault. While criticizing the Hollywood movement, Burke also acknowledged the work they were doing.

established the civil or anti-civil profile of redress toward women. Supporters of the French manifesto pointed out that women should not always play the role of victims. While recognizing that women also seduce, they called for the relativization of harassment. The latter should be judged as the situational process in which a man and a woman relate to each other. For their part, those who supported *#Metoo*, insisted on considering the normative framework that defines the social and legal meaning of harassment.

Autre Parole called to judge each case of harassment according to a particular context in order to determine the guilt of the harasser and the responsibility of the harassed, which aroused the criticism of those who supported *#Metoo*, who warned that such a position violated from the outset reparation to the victim. Finally, the dispute discussed the role of the body as a determinant of the feminine. For *Autre Parole*, the body, even if it has been subjected to violence and humiliation, cannot determine women's destiny. According to this position, harassment is not relevant to freedom of spirit. Supporters of *#Metoo* charged that this judgment ignores the relevance of the body in the lives of women, as well as men.

The dispute that *Autre Parole* unleashed within public opinion in the face of *#Metoo*'s positions revealed the varying interpretations of harassment, its prevention, and its attention. The competing discourses made it possible to observe a defined set of binary codes on a global scale that sought to interpret the position of U.S. and French female actors. These binary codes made it possible to observe that there is concern on an international scale about harassment and violence against women, ready to be signified in order to understand and thereby generate the mechanisms of prevention and reparation to the victims. There was also a concern about who the perpetrators are, what mechanisms of power and relationships they respond to, as well as the motives behind their actions. The sexual drive, the body, and the agency of men and women were all part of these debates. The contested discourses imputed to *#Metoo* and *Autre Parole* qualities such as language, race, gender, social class, and ethnicity in order to attribute to them civic vices and virtues. In addition, a process of geographic and temporal moral dichotomization of the representatives of each movement was established: depending on their geographic location and generational ascription, a certain moral purity or impurity was attributed to each proposal.

As can be seen in Tables 3.1 and 3.2, the ways of classifying what civil or authentic or anti-civil and inauthentic feminism means can vary based on whether *#Metoo* or *Autre Parole* is endorsed. Table 3.1 shows that those who supported *#Metoo* established the criteria of civility and authenticity of feminism based on skin color, class or status, and age. They also took into account how they valued the relationship between men and women (symmetrical or asymmetrical), the harassment itself (as domination or seduction), their position on denunciation (public or through legal frameworks), and whether or not the presumption of innocence for the alleged harasser should be established.

Table 3.2 shows how *Autre Parole* classified the civility and authenticity of feminism according to the relationship between the body and the spirit of women, its

Table 3.1 Civil/anti-civil attribution since *#Metoo*

	Race	Class/ Status	Age	Female to male ratio	Harassment	Complaint	Presumption of innocence
Civil/ authentic feminism	Non-white	Medium/ Low	Youth	Asymmetric	Domination	Public	No
Anti-civil/ inauthentic feminism	White	High	Older	Symmetrical	Seduction	Legal	Yes

Source: Own elaboration

evaluation of eroticism (whether as a game or a power relationship), and the consideration of the exercise of sexuality (marked by freedom or by a puritanical vision), and, finally. Whether or not the relationship between men and women is symmetrical. In a similar way, it is taken into consideration whether the complaint should be legal and secret or public, as well as whether or not the presumption of innocence of the alleged harasser is positively valued.

The debate within public opinion on *Autre Parole* and *#Metoo* expressed that certain conflicts and social tensions were discussed at a differentiated level, not exclusively on a local scale, but globally. Certainly, the comments in front of the competing positions did not discard the particularities of European or Latin American countries, but there is the idea that it was possible to build—with their particularities—mechanisms of containment and reparation for the damage caused by harassment. In this sense, the dispute between *Autre Parole* and *#Metoo* made it possible to notice the presence of a civil discourse on a global scale.

We believe that if the debate on harassment is global, it is because there is a quest to build more equitable and egalitarian relationships between men and women. *#Metoo* has not been an event that faded in time, its spirit crystallized in Mexico, as in other Latin American countries, with a series of denunciations in the artistic, political, academic and communication worlds. The response included the support and backing of thousands of women to those who dared to denounce the harassment. However, the movements also triggered a response from men and women who supported the arguments set forth in *Autre Parole*. This fact should capture our attention: the narratives, as well as the imputations on those who participated in the debate, despite the particularities of the national context, maintained similar patterns of interpretation and meaning. However, for the Mexican case, as will be seen below, was mediated at times by presidential power, giving rise to the emergence of new semantics on the meaning of harassment, anonymous denunciations, burdens of proof, as well as the meaning of feminism.

Table 3.2 Civil/anti-civil attribution from *Autre Parole*

	Essence female	Eroticism	Sexuality	Female to male ratio	Harassment	Complaint	Presumption of innocence
Civil/authentic feminism	Body	Game	Free	Symmetrical	Seduction	Legal	Yes
Anti-civil/inauthentic feminism	Spirit	Power of attorney	Puritan	Asymmetric (women as "eternal girls")	Domination	Public	No

Source: Own elaboration

References

Amo, A. (2018, February 1). The feminist awakening in France. *Rebellion.* https://rebelion.org/el-despertar-feminista-en-francia/

Andrade, F. (2018, January 29). Un psiquiatra por favor. *NTR Zacatecas.* http://ntrzacatecas.com/2018/01/29/relatos-de-la-historia-patria-153/

Associate Press (AP) (2018, March 06). #YoTambién grows although sometimes its impact is minimal. *La Jornada.* http://www.jornada.unam.mx/ultimas/2018/03/06/crece-yotambien-aunque-a-veces-su-impacto-es-minimo-4662.html

Atwood, M. (2018, January 15). Am I a bad feminist. *The Globe and Mail.* https://www.theglobeandmail.com/opinion/am-i-a-bad-feminist/article37591823/

Ayuso, S. (2018, January 12). The frontiers (and limits?) of feminism. *El País.* https://elpais.com/internacional/2018/01/12/actualidad/1515766831_721634.html

Belaich, C. (2018, January 11). La "séduction à la française" est-elle en danger? *Libération.* https://www.liberation.fr/france/2018/01/11/la-seduction-a-la-francaise-est-elle-en-danger_1621717

Beltran, R. (2018, January 23). Sexual harassment to the fore. *Vanguardia.* https://vanguardia.com.mx/articulo/el-acoso-sexual-primer-plano

Bernal-Triviño, A. (2018, January 10). It's not puritanism, it's machismo. *El Periódico.* https://www.elperiodico.com/es/opinion/20180110/no-es-puritanismo-es-machismo-articulo-ana-i-bernal-trivino-6543390

Berrin, D. (2017, December 22). Should we forgive the men who assaulted us. *The New York Times.* https://www.nytimes.com/2017/12/22/opinion/metoo-sexual-assault-orgiveness.html.

Cadei, E. (2017, October 25). Few in Washington are saying #MeToo. California congresswoman wants to change that. *Miami Herald.* https://web.archive.org/web/20171026054331/http:/www.miamiherald.com/news/politics-government/article180767911.html

Carlson, G. & Carlson, G. (2017, October 10). How to encourage more women to report sexual harassment. *The New York Times.* https://www.nytimes.com/2017/10/10/opinion/women-reporting-sexual-harassment.html.

Casanova, A. (2018, January 26). Importuning is not right. *Cima News.* http://www.cimacnoticias.com.mx/noticia/importunar-no-es-derecho.

Coll, A. (2018, January 16). Clumsy seduction or harassment? *The Empty Chair.* https://www.lasillavacia.com/red-de-expertos/red-de-las-mujeres/seduccion-torpe-o-acoso/

Collado, A. (2018, January 27). Exaggerated, persigned and also whores, just in case. *The Broken Chair.* https://lasillarota.com/opinion/columnas/exageradas-persignadas-y-tambien-putas-por-si-acaso/202271

Collins, L. (2018, January 10). Why did Catherine Deneuve and other prominent French women denounce #MeToo? *The New Yorker* https://www.newyorker.com/news/daily-comment/why-did-catherine-deneuve-and-other-prominent-frenchwomen-denounce-metoo

Cruz, P. (2018, January 17). Atwood VS. #metoo: Against the triumph of populist justice. *La Razón.* https://www.larazon.es/cultura/atwood-vs-metoo-contra-el-triunfo-de-la-justicia-populista-NG17449510

De la Barreda, L. (2018, January 25). Abuse versus seduction. *Excelsior.* https://www.excelsior.com.mx/opinion/luis-de-la-barreda-solorzano/2018/01/25/1215904.

De la Peña, A. (2018, January 14). #MeToo or there isn't that much anger. *El Sol de México.* https://www.elsoldemexico.com.mx/análisis/metoo-o-nohaytantabronca-562069.html

De Paz, M. (2018, January 23). MeToo: Analyzing a controversy that rocks Hollywood. *El Comercio.* https://elcomercio.pe/luces/impreso-metoo-analizando-polemica-remece-hollywood-noticia-491123

Díaz, S. (2018, January 20). Debate: Argentine women, closer to #Metoo than French women. *Clarín.* https://www.clarin.com/sociedad/debate-argentinas-cerca-metoo-francesas_0_ByQds4ZBG.html

Dresser, D. (2018, January 15). Torquemadas. *El Siglo de Durango,* https://www.elsiglodedurango.com.mx/noticia/933603.torquemadas.html.

Dudda, R. (2018, February 1). Against Anglo-Saxon hegemony. *El País*. https://elpais.com/elpais/2018/02/01/opinion/1517508501_062344.html

Dunham, L. (2017, October 9). Lena Dunham: Harvey Weinstein and the silence of the men. *The New York Times*. https://www.nytimes.com/2017/10/09/opinion/harvey-weinstein-lena-dunham-silence-.html

D'Zurilla, C. (2017, October 16). In saying #MeToo, Alyssa Milano pushes awareness campaign about sexual assault and harassment. *Los Angeles Times*. https://web.archive.org/web/20171017075641/http:/www.latimes.com/entertainment/la-et-entertainment-news-updates-metoo-campaign-me-too-alyssa-milano-1508173882-tmlstory.html

Estremadoiro, W. (2018, January 19). Extremes on the issue of sexual harassment. *Los Tiempos*.

Europa Press. (2018, January 11). Femen defends 'me too' against women like French artists, who "play into the hands of the patriarchy". *El Periódico*. https://www.elperiodico.com/es/ocio-y-cultura/20180111/femen-defiende-el-me-too-frente-a-mujeres-como-las-artistas-francesas-que-hacen-el-juego-al-patriarcado-6545583

Faur, E. (2018, January 16). Sexual abuse. Stop the hand. *Anfibia Magazine*. https://www.revista-anfibia.com/parar-la-mano-2/.

Faus, J. (2018, January 1). More than 300 Hollywood women create fund for sexual harassment victims. *El País*. https://elpais.com/cultura/2018/01/01/actualidad/1514844114_604793.html

Félix, P. (2018, January 18). From puritanism to reality. *El Universal*. http://www.eluniversal.com.mx/articulo/paola-felix-diaz/nación/del-puritanismo-la-realidad.

Fernández, L. (2018, January 26). Enjoyment versus puritanism, still? *Clarín*. https://www.clarin.com/revista-enie/ideas/goce-versus-puritanismo-todavia_0_BkzGAWYHM.html

Ferreyra, M. (2018, February 2). Growing up after the storm. *La Razón*. https://www.razon.com.mx/crecer-después-la-tormenta/.

Filipovic, J. (2017, November 24). The Bad News on 'Good' Girls. *The New York Times*. https://www.nytimes.com/2017/11/24/opinion/sunday/girls-parents-boys-gender.html.

France Télévisions. (2018, January 10). TRIBUNE. "Les porcs et leurs allié.e.s ont raison de s'inquiéter": Caroline De Haas et des militantes féministes répondent à la tribune publiée dans "Le Monde". *Franceinfo*. https://www.francetvinfo.fr/societe/droits-des-femmes/tribune-les-porcs-et-leurs-allie-e-s-ont-raison-de-sinquieter-caroline-de-haas-et-des-militantes-feministes-repondent-a-la-tribune-publiee-dans-le-monde_2553497.html

García, B. (2018, January 28). What do we talk about when we talk about harassment. *Mujer Hoy*. http://www.mujerhoy.com/vivir/sexo-pareja/201801/28/acoso-sexual-movimiento-metoo-20180125181212.html

Gérard, A. (2018, January 11). Débat: faut-il défendre "la liberté d'importuner"? *Le Parisen*. http://www.leparisien.fr/societe/debat-faut-il-defendre-la-liberte-d-importuner-11-01-2018-7494240.php

Gersen, J. (2017, December 20). The transformation of sexual-harassment law will be double-faced. *The New Yorker*. https://www.newyorker.com/news/news-desk/the-transformation-of-sexual-harassment-law-will-be-double-faced.

Gill, C. (2018, January 12). This McCarthyite campaign against men goes too far. *The Times*. https://www.thetimes.co.uk/article/this-mccarthyite-campaign-against-men-goes-too-far-dnsphx9s3

González, A. (2018, January 13). From bullying to puritanism. Milenio. http://www.milenio.com/firmas/ariel_gonzalez_jimenez/acoso-puritanismo-feminismo-metoo-hollywood-globos_oro-catherine_deneuve_18_1102869742.html

Hill, Z. (2017, October 20). Black woman Tarana burke founded the 'me too' movement long before hastags. *The New York Times*. https://www.nytimes.com/2017/10/20/us/me-too-movement-tarana-burke.html

Hubbard, S. (2017, December 15). Russell Simmons, R. Kelly, and why black women can't say #MeToo. *The New York Times*. https://www.nytimes.com/2017/12/15/opinion/russell-simmons-black-women-metoo.html

Kislinger, L. (2018, January 24). One hundred French women said… *Efecto Cocuyo*. http://efecto-cocuyo.com/opinion/cien-francesas-dijeron/

Kivisto, P., & Sciortino, G. (2015). Introduction: Thinking the civil sphere. In P. Kivisto & G. Sciortino (Eds.), *Solidarity, justice and incorporation* (pp. 1–30). Oxford University Press.

La Voz de Galicia. (2018, January 14). The border between flirting and sexual harassment. *La Voz de Galicia*. https://www.lavozdegalicia.es/noticia/sociedad/2018/01/14/frontera-flirteo-acoso-sexual/0003_201801G14P25991.htm.

Lamas, M. (2018). *Harassment. legitimate denunciation or victimization?* Fondo de Cultura Económica.

Latapí, A. (2018, January 18). From witches to inquisitors? *Milenio*. https://www.milenio.com/opinion/alejandra-latapi/columna-alejandra-latapi/de-brujas-a-inquisidoras

Lehoux, V. (2018, January 13). Laure Adler: Pourquoi je n'ai pas signé la tribune sur 'la liberté d'importuner'. *Télérama*, https://www.telerama.fr/monde/laure-adler-pourquoi-je-nai-pas-signe-la-tribune-sur-la-liberte-dimportuner,n5437559.php

Lévy-Willard, A. (2018, January 11). Nous voulons être importunées sexuellement!. *Libération*. http://annette.blogs.liberation.fr/2018/01/11/xxx/

Lozada, L. (2018, January 14). Neither so much that it burns the Saint, nor so much that it does not illuminate him. *Milenio*. http://www.milenio.com/firmas/luis_lozada_leon/le_monde-acoso_sexual-metoo-catherine_deneuve-donald_trump_18_1103469691.html

Lucario, S. (2018a, January 10). 'Disappointing', 'sexist' but also 'understandable' and 'debatable'? Mexican women respond to French feminist manifesto. *The Huffington Post*. http://www.huffingtonpost.com.mx/2018/01/10/decepcionante-machista-pero-tambien-entendible-y-debatible-mexicanas-responden-al-manifiesto-feminista-frances_a_23330262/

Lucario, S. (2018b, January 12). Fernanda Solórzano: 'Contains statements that can be problematic'. *The Huffington Post*. https://www.huffingtonpost.com.mx/2018/01/12/fernanda-solorzano-contiene-afirmaciones-que-pueden-ser-problematicas_a_23332098/

Lucario, S. (2018c, January 14). Karla Michelle Salas: 'Abuse of power is not natural, violence is not natural'. *The Huffington Post*. http://www.huffingtonpost.com.mx/2018/01/14/karla-michelle-salas-el-abuso-de-poder-no-es-natural-la-violencia-no-es-natural_a_23332155/

Lucario, S. (2018d, January 14). Martha Tagle: It represents a valuable opportunity to continue talking about the issue of sexual harassment and sexual harassment. *The Huffington Post*. https://www.huffingtonpost.com.mx/2018/01/14/martha-tagle-representa-una-valiosa-oportunidad-para-seguir-hablando-de-la-problematica-del-acoso-y-hostigamiento-sexual_a_23332281/

Lucario, S. (2018e, January 14). Regina Tamés: "We women must treasure and take care of the sexual freedoms we have achieved". *The Huffington Post*. http://www.huffingtonpost.com.mx/2018/01/14/regina-tames-las-mujeres-debemos-atesorar-y-cuidar-las-libertades-sexuales-que-hemos-logrado_a_23332235/

Lucario, S. (2018f, January 14). Tamara de Anda: 'French feminists who signed the manifesto don't see beyond their noses'. *The Huffington Post*. http://www.huffingtonpost.com.mx/2018/01/14/tamara-de-anda-las-feministas-francesas-que-firmaron-el-manifiesto-no-ven-mas-alla-de-sus-narices_a_23332146/

Lucario, S. (2018g, January 12). Ximena Andión: "it is risky to think that any gallantry or seduction is harassment". *The Huffington Post*. http://www.huffingtonpost.com.mx/2018/01/12/fernanda-solorzano-contiene-afirmaciones-que-pueden-ser-problematicas_a_23332098/

Madrid, A. (2018, January 16). Open war on the piropo: The tweet that sweeps Twitter. *Los 40*. http://los40.com/los40/2018/01/16/bigbang/1516116247_222282.html

Marco, J. (2018, January 13). Moral panic. *José María Marco*. https://www.josemariamarco.com/ideas-ideas/panico-moral/.

Martínez, L. (2018, January 13). Notes on the discussion around the #MeToo movement. *The Economist*. https://www.eleconomista.com.mx/política/Apuntes-sobre-la-discusion-alrededor-del-movimiento-MeToo-20180113-0001.html

Mascia, C. (2018, January 15). The feminist war is waged in the media. *El País*. https://elpais.com/elpais/2018/01/12/opinion/1515788449_947888.html.

Melgar, L. (2018, January 22). Bullying is not up for debate II/II. *The Economist*. https://www.eleconomista.com.mx/opinion/El-acoso-no-esta-a-debate%2D%2D20180122-0046.html

Méndez, J. (2018, January 14). INDICIO ESMERALDA: #MeToo the man as enemy. *The East.* http://www.eloriente.net/home/2018/01/14/indicio-esmeralda-metoo/

Merino, O. (2018, January 20). French women and the #MeToo. *El Periódico.* https://www.elperiodico.com/es/opinion/20180120/las-francesas-y-el-metoo-articulo-olga-merino-acoso-sexual-6566279

Merkin, D. (2018, January 5). Publicly, we say #MeToo. Privately, we have misgivings. *The New York Times.* https://www.nytimes.com/2018/01/05/opinion/golden-globes-metoo.html

Morejón, R. (2018, January 17). Other women with a voice: Truthfulness, sex and freedom. *Diario Vasco.* https://www.diariovasco.com/opinion/mujeres-veracidad-sexo-20180117212412-nt.html

Munker, B. (2018, January 19). The #MeToo movement hits Sundance: 'Now, men's role is to listen,' says Redford.' *El Mundo.* http://www.elmundo.es/cultura/cine/2018/01/19/5a61e317e2704e91448b462d.html

Mural de Negro. (2018, January 15). Lydia Cacho: 'Gallantry and seduction involve a game'. *Mural de Negro,* http://muraldegenero.com/lydia-cacho-la-galanteria-la-seduccion-implican-juego/

Nebot, M. (2018, January 11). Mud wrestling among feminists? No thanks. *Public.* http://blogs.publico.es/otrasmiradas/12312/lucha-en-el-barro-entre-feministas-no-gracias/

Neill, U. (2017). When scientists say, "me, too." *Scientific American.* Advance online publication.

Ohlheiser, A. (2017, October 19). The woman behind 'Me Too' knew the power of the phrase when she created it 10 years ago. *Los Angeles Times.* https://web.archive.org/web/20240907032717/https://www.washingtonpost.com/news/the-intersect/wp/2017/10/19/the-woman-behind-me-too-knew-the-power-of-the-phrase-when-she-created-it-10-years-ago/?utm_term=.bc28f8815787

Olavarría, E. (2018, January 31). French men raise their voices in favor of #MeToo. *France 24.* https://www.france24.com/es/20180131-hombres-franceses-metoo

Peker, L. (2018, January 19). Neither puritanical, nor pure victims. *Página 12.* https://www.pagina12.com.ar/90035-ni-puritanas-ni-puras-victimas

Podirier, A. (2018, January 19). Deneuve and the feminism of French women. *El País.* https://elpais.com/elpais/2018/01/19/opinion/1516380216_568037.html

Priego-Broca, M. (2018, January 16). How to march together. *The Broken Chair.* https://lasillarota.com/opinion/columnas/2018/1/16/como-marchar-juntas-342195.html

Raulin, N., Mallaval, C. & Bretton, L. (2018, March 20). Marlène Schiappa: un ovni pour la galaxie féministe. *Libération.* https://www.liberation.fr/politiques/2018/03/20/marlene-schiappa-un-ovni-pour-la-galaxie-feministe_1637682

Razer, H. (2018, October 11). The 'black gown' Golden globes 'inspired' no one but the empty-headed stars in them. *Daily Review.* https://dailyreview.com.au/author/helen-razer/

Revuelta, L. (2018, January 28). The cultural and social revolution of #MeToo. *ABC.* http://www.abc.es/cultura/cultural/abci-revolucion-cultural-y-social-metoo-201801280121_noticia.html

Rodríguez, A. (2018, January 26). #MeToo: Declaration of war. *Letras Libres.* https://www.letraslibres.com/espana-mexico/cultura/metoo-declaracion-guerra

RTBF. (2018, January 11). *Anne Morelli: "Les femmes paraissent toujours victimes, mais nous sommes aussi dragueuses".* RTBF. https://www.rtbf.be/info/societe/detail_anne-morelli-les-femmes-paraissent-toujours-victimes-mais-nous-sommes-aussi-dragueuses?id=9808351

Ruiz, C. (2018, January 11). #MeToo goes against harassment, not flirting: Specialists. *Milenio.* http://www.milenio.com/tendencias/marta-lamas-catalina-ruiz-navarro-me-too-francesas-acoso-sexual_0_1101490031.html

Russonello, G. (2018, January, 6). Read Oprah Winfrey's Golden Globes speech. *The New York Times.* https://www.google.com/search?q=traductor&rlz=1C1CHBD_esMX1163MX1163&oq=tr&gs_lcrp=EgZjaHJvbWUqDggAEEUYJxg7GIAEGIoFMg4IABBBFGCcYOxiABBiKBTIGCAEQRRhAMgYIAhBFGDkyDAgDECMYJxiABBiKBTISCAQQABhDGIMBGGLEDGIAEGIoFMgYIBRBFGD0yBggGEEUYPDIGCAcQRRg80gEIMjQ1MWowajeoAgCwAgA&sourceid=chrome&ie=UTF-8.

Salvador, Á. (2018, January 13). American vs. French women: History of an old rivalry that returned after sexual harassment allegations in Hollywood. *Clarín*. https://www.clarin.com/opinion/marilyn-vs-brigitte-norteamericanas-francesas-volvieron-ring-fenomeno-metoo_0_Sk3f6CPNM.html

Sánchez-Mellado, L. (2018, January 10). Paz, sisters. *El País*, https://elpais.com/elpais/2018/01/10/opinion/1515602350_010954.html

Sénac, R. (2018, January 12). L'enjeu est que chacun.e puisse s'imaginer comme une semblable. *Le Noveau Magazine*. https://www.nouveau-magazine-litteraire.com/idees/-lenjeu-est-que-chacun-puisse-simaginer-comme-un-semblable-

Stephens, B. (2017, December 20). When #MeToo goes too far. *The New York Times*. https://www.nytimes.com/2017/12/20/opinion/metoo-damon-too-far.html

The Boston Globe. (2017, October 17). *Where'd the "Me Too" initiative really come from? Activist Tarana Burke, long before hashtags.* The Boston Globe. https://www.bostonglobe.com/lifestyle/2017/10/17/alyssa-milano-credits-activist-tarana-burke-with-founding-metoo-movement-years-ago/o2Jv29v6ljObkKPTPB9KGP/story.html#:~:text=Burke%20wrote%20that%20the%20 "me,met%20Heaven%2C"%20Burke%20said

Thomas, F. (2018, January 24). Untangling the splash. *El Tiempo*. https://www.eltiempo.com/opinion/columnistas/florence-thomas/desenredar-el-salpicon-el-debate-del-acoso-sexual-174388

Toranian, V. (2018, January 15). Libération sexuelle: une autre parole est-elle possible? *Revue Des Deux Mondes*. https://www.revuedesdeuxmondes.fr/liberation-sexuelle-parole-possible/

Torreblanca, C., Meltis, M., Zilli, M., Soria, J., Tejas, D., Philipson, D. & MacGregor, C. (2018, January 19). Feminism is not the new Puritanism. *Animal Politico*. https://www.animalpolitico.com/blogueros-blog-invitado/2018/01/19/feminismo-no-nuevo-puritanismo/.

Viennot, B. (2018, January 15). Pourquoi j'ai signé la tribune "Des femmes libèrent une autre parole". *Slate*. https://www.slate.fr/story/156254/debat-feminisme-pourquoi-tribune-femmes-autre-parole

Weiss, B. (2018, January 15). Aziz Ansari Is Guilty. Of Not Being a Mind Reader. *The New York Times*. https://www.nytimes.com/2018/01/15/opinion/aziz-ansari-babe-sexual-harassment.html.

West, L. (2018, January 17). Aziz, we tried to warn you. *The New York Times*. https://www.nytimes.com/2018/01/17/opinion/aziz-ansari-metoo-sex.html.

Wiener, G. (2018a, January 20). The French women's manifesto is a revenge of the patriarchy. *The Republic*. http://larepublica.pe/domingo/1173741-el-manifiesto-de-las-francesas-es-una-venganza-del-patriarcado.

Wiener, G. (2018b, January 13). I stalk you, 'moi non plus'. *The New York Times*. https://www.nytimes.com/es/2018/01/13/yo-te-acoso-moi-non-plus/

Zárate, L. (2018, January 16). #MeToo deserves to go beyond mediatized denunciations. *Las 2 Orillas*. https://www.las2orillas.co/metoo-merece-ir-mas-alla-de-denuncias-mediatizadas/#google_vignette

Chapter 4
Heroes, Villains and the Textbook Sexist

Abstract This chapter examines the controversy surrounding the legitimacy of #MT in calling for sanctions and reparations for women in the Mexican context. It illustrates how debates that oversimplify the roles of actors within civil society undermine the development of a crucial democratic center. First, the chapter outlines the rise of #MT as a powerful civil movement in public opinion, highlighting a key incident involving a well-known rock musician who died by suicide after facing harassment allegations. The analysis then explores how #MT evaluated presidential legitimacy, particularly concerning the appointment of an individual with close ties to the president, who has been accused of harassment during their time as ambassador to Panama.

Keywords Public opinion · Presidential power · #MeToo México · Public office · Social power · Social power

4.1   *#Metoo* in Mexico

The *#Metoo* (*#MT*) in the United States brought the problem of harassment in the workplace into the global media spotlight. Its actions even strengthened legal reforms to sanction this practice in the United States and other countries (Rhode, 2019). When #Metoo first arrived in Mexico, it did not generate much resonance, even though harassment is a serious problem for millions of women in the country (Frías, 2019; Sánchez, 2020; McLean, 2020).[1] However, by March of 2019, 2000

---

[1] According to the National Survey on the Dynamics of Household Relationships (2016), *19.2 million women were subjected at some point in their lives to some type of intimidation, harassment, stalking or sexual abuse. However, the data from this survey do not allow us to appreciate the*

45

L. A. Cardona Acuña, N. Arteaga Botello, *Feminism, Power and Public Opinion in Mexico*, SpringerBriefs in Sociology,
https://doi.org/10.1007/978-3-032-14141-5_4

complaints were registered on social networks with the hashtag #MeToo (Nicolas-Gavilan et al., 2019), and the phenomenon unleashed a confrontation within public opinion about its meaning. Two competing interpretations were generated in terms of the binary coding of civil discourse. The first interpretation justified anonymous denunciation as an appropriate way to demand reparation for the damages caused by harassment. A second interpretation justified the annoyance and weariness of women in the face of harassment, although it qualified the anonymous complaint mechanism as inadequate, without evidence and assuming *de facto* the guilt of the accused. From the second perspective, it was judged that #Metoo was contaminated from the beginning since it functioned as judge and party at the same time.

This chapter examines the dispute around the legitimacy of #MT to denounce, and to demand sanction and redress for women in the Mexican case. Two moments are analyzed, in which #MT was equated with the actions of men who allegedly committed acts of aggression or violence against women with the anti-civil referents of civil discourse. The first moment describes the strength with which #MT began as a civil power as regards public opinion, until a well-known rock musician committed suicide after being accused of harassment. This event generated debate within public opinion about #MT's strategies of denunciation. Those who defended denunciation through the *hashtag*, described it as a mobilizer of civil power, made up of conscious, informed, autonomous, and critical activists and victims, driven by the desire to change things. Those who criticized the movement assessed it as impure, pointing out that, although justified, its spirit had been contaminated by women trapped by rancor and revenge, who were far from seeking justice. Finally, there were those who opposed #MT—despite the need to act against harassment—asserting that its promoters were irrational, reckless, and impervious to self-criticism, in other words, anti-civil.

The second moment was marked by the appointment by the president of a person close to him as ambassador to Panama. This moment reacted to #MT by bringing to account the alleged acts of harassment that the newly appointed ambassador had committed when he was a professor in an institution of higher education in Mexico. The president defended his appointment and accused #MT of being representative of conservatism and reactionary opposition. This event sparked a debate within public opinion concerning those who questioned and those who supported the president's ambassadorial appointment. The former considered that the president had not fulfilled his office, failing in the institution that has a universalist understanding of the organization of authority. Those who supported the president assumed that, as an embodiment of civilian power, he could establish the anti-civilian character of the plaintiffs. Panama rejected the appointment of the Mexican ambassador, which

---

dynamics of harassment in the work environment. Nevertheless, the information provided by the federal public administration on harassment cases in government is a good reference to understand the scope of the problem. According to public data, in 2017, 145 complaints were registered among federal public administration officials for alleged cases of harassment or sexual harassment (INMUJERES, 2017, p. 13). In 2018, the figure was 211 complaints (INMUJERES; SFP, CONAVIM, 2018, p. 15).

was interpreted by the president's critics as a triumph of feminism on a regional scale, while the president charged that the appointment of the official was rejected by Panama's foreign minister without the approval of the country's president, which unleashed harsh criticism of López Obrador by Panamanian officials who considered his statement proof of his machismo.

One of the first expressions of #MeToo in Mexico manifested through #Yaestuvo in 2017, organized by women dedicated to comedy. By the end of that year, it featured more than 100 complaints.[2] In that same year, other movements emerged in social networks under tags such as #NoEsNormal, #NiUnaMas, #NiUnaMenos, #MeToo, or #YoTambién.[3] In 2018, journalist Carmen Aristegui presented several cases of harassment victims.[4] The allegations were challenged and the women who offered their testimonies suffered serious aggression on social networks. This gave rise to the #Yonodenuncioporque movement, with which the obstacles to denouncing harassment against women were evidenced.

A year later, on March 21, 2019, Anna G. González accused writer Herson Barona of beating several women and asked other victims of the writer to make public complaints.[5] The accused denied the allegations made against him. Gonzalez's complaint was replicated using #Metoo to point out cases of harassment in the circles of art, science, communication, and academia. On March 22, the #Metooescritoremexicanos emerged, along with the account @metooescritores, through which alleged harassers in the literary guild were denounced. From this account, different tags were created to denounce harassment, sexual violence, as well as to demand women's labor rights. Little by little more accounts were added, including: @MeTooCineMx, @MeTooPeriodista, @MeTooCreativos, @metoomusicamx, @MeTooFotografos, @metooartesmx, @MeTooEmpresario, @metootechmx, @MeTooAbogadosMx, @MeTooMedicina, @MeTooActivista1, @metootuiteros, @metooteatromx, @MeTooJalisco, @MeTooAcademicos, @MeTooPoliticos, @MeTooAgenciasMx, and @MeTooCulturaMex. Similarly, public and private universities in the country installed "clotheslines against harassment," a practice adopted for several years that consisted of displaying the names of alleged harassers with a description of the situations of aggression in visible places on campus.

The media highlighted that the denunciations through the Mexican #Metoo in 2018 were circumscribed to the entertainment industry (Nicolas-Gavilan et al., 2019). However, by 2019, it expanded to other spaces such as music, academia, and other sectors considered in the view of the movement as alien to the dynamics of harassment due to an apparent more open and liberal position regarding issues of sexuality (Peñaloza, 2019a; Maza, 2019; Fuentes, 2019; Zamarrón, 2019a; Vela,

---

[2] AP Agency (2017, November 28).

[3] Fundar Centro de Análisis (2017). Contra la violencia que no se ve.

[4] Redacción AN (2020, March 8).

[5] Avila (2019).

2019). As the movement gained momentum, voices for and against it emerged within public opinion.

Those in favor of #Metoo emphasized the need to continue with the denunciations to drive a feminist revolution (Maza, 2019), and other women were invited to break the silence, point out the harassers, and bring them to justice (Vela, 2019; Peñaloza, 2019a). Some journalists believed that all denunciations should be considered as true, without doubting the facts narrated by the victims (Peñaloza, 2019a). To the extent that there were more denunciations, it would be possible to understand how Mexican society related to sex, desire, and frustration, necessary inputs to push for social transformation (Zamarrón, 2019a; Fuentes, 2019). Likewise, those in favor of the movement considered that the #Metoo denunciations had made it possible to show the inability of justice institutions to attend to victims of sexual harassment or violence (Vela, 2019; Fuentes, 2019).

The positions against the #MeToo mobilization warned that some testimonies pointed directly to their harasser, leaving behind anonymity. From this position, it was considered that some accusations were motivated by spite and anger with the ex-partner, or by the intention to defame the accused (Guarneros, 2019). In this way, it was interpreted that the wave of harassment accusations placed #Metoo in the media, due to the fact that people who were already known to harass women were denounced, while new alleged harassers or abusers emerged (Peñaloza, 2019a). These commentators suggested that denunciations in some workspaces, such as educational spaces, were leaving *Twitter* to crystallize into clotheslines and normative procedures of a labor nature, in the form of a new application of justice.

The complaints on social networks revealed physical aggression, looks considered lewd, inappropriate touching, intimidation, abuse, and pressure to obtain sexual favors in exchange for winning a position or a promotion at work, improving a qualification or income, or obtaining a role in a film. Some defendants accepted responsibility and offered apologies; others did not. There were defendants who were sanctioned or reprimanded, others were fired, removed, or forced to resign from their jobs (Rivera, 2020). Most of the accused lost their prestige and authority, regardless of whether due process and application of justice was followed, that is, without the intervention of regulatory institutions. Faced with this wave of denunciations, some news columns suggested that it was necessary to analyze their context, and the sanctions applied to the alleged harassers. As some journalists pointed out, "[U]nless it is judicially punishable, it would be prudent to take this [the complaints] more as an exercise of red lights. Not as a lynching, but as a look to the future: to be careful with certain people, to hope that this discourages abusers or makes them change" (Peñaloza, 2019a).

Among the accused, the name of a renowned artist emerged, who a few days after his appearance on social networks, ended his life. The suicide of the musician Vega-Gil, member of a famous rock band called Botellita de Jerez, added one more element to this dispute: the alleged responsibility of #Metoo for the death of the musician.

4.2 *#Metoo Vis-a-Vis* **Suicide**

On March 31, 2019, Armando Vega-Gil, member of the rock band Botellita de Jerez and writer of children's books and stories, was accused, via @metoomusicamx.[6] A 27-year-old woman accused him of having invited her to his home 14 years earlier, when she was 13 years old, and of having made her feel uncomfortable with a series of sexual advances. According to the alleged victim, Vega-Gil took advantage of his fame as a musician to obtain her phone number when she approached him for an autograph and a photograph at a concert: "He took advantage of my naivety and cajoled me […] He told me that I was different from those of my age, that I was very special."[7] The complainant pointed out that the musician had invited her to his house, where she went with a friend, and there, he took pictures of them which made them feel very uncomfortable because "he asked us to get comfortable and everything."[8] She shared her feeling of discomfort and the alleged messages Vega-Gil was sending her by harassing her: "He was telling me more and more disgusting and explicitly sexual things until I got really scared; I decided to block him and change my phone."[9] The victim warned:

> If I had had an ounce more innocence and had gone to his house alone, I am sure that old man would have abused me […] I am sure I am not the only one […] The man writes books for children and teenagers, and they are stories that if you know the perverse side of the author, are very sinister.[10]

Vega-Gil denied the accusations. He pointed out that he was a public person and that he constantly received many minors in his home […] "and I maintain communication with them."[11] The musician stated, "I write songs for minors, and I am a parent who actively supports the defense of the universal rights of children." Recognizing the legitimate nature of the anonymous complaint, Vega-Gil pointed out that he had invited the victim to talk about the matter, she with evidence and witnesses, and accompanied by advisors and the girls of #MetooMúsicosMexicanos, so that she would be sure that there would be no threats and reprisals.[12] The musician defended the movement, as well as the right of women to denounce their aggressors. But he warned that, with the denunciation against him, everything was lost to him: his work

---

[6] The account @metoomusicamx presented itself with the following description: "An open space to denounce aggressions in the music industry. Send a DM with your anonymous complaint and we will publish the name of the aggressor." MetooMúsicosMexicanos (2019, April 1). Published on *Twitter*. Retrieved from https://Twitter.com/mariomonroymmty/status/1112821091314094080/photo/1.

[7] Bridges Glz. (2019, April 1). Posted on *Twitter*. Retrieved from https://Twitter.com/PuentesGlz/status/1112765475585474562/photo/1.

[8] Ibid.

[9] Ibid.

[10] Ibid.

[11] Vega Gil (2019, April 1).

[12] Ibid.

and his public image. So, he announced via Twitter that he would commit suicide, warning not to blame anyone for his decision (Rodríguez et al., 2019). He finally offered an apology to women if at some point he had offended them with his macho ways, and assured that "machos, we are creatures of our times."[13] Vega-Gil's lifeless body was found hanging a few hours later from a tree near his home.

Once the musician's death was made public, the #MetooMúsicosMexicanos account reported that they had spoken with Vega-Gil to talk, but that they had no answer, only a suicide letter for which, they claimed, he knew he was guilty: "It was media blackmail."[14] They said that the musician's death was his responsibility and no one else's. The account disappeared a few hours later, and its administrators announced that it had been hacked to remove them from the network, warning: "We will not be silent. Now more than ever, we continue to support the victims and those who still do not dare to raise their voices."[15] They asserted that they had been harmed and attacked by the media, "who tried to make us feel as if Armando Vega-Gil's death was our fault. We did not kill him. It was a suicide. Know that this is also violence, and you don't notice it because it is normalized."[16] The account later reappeared but closed permanently on April 3. The last post read:

> We deeply regret the suicide of Armando Vega Gil. Our initial reaction was not appropriate and, therefore, we extend an honest apology to all those close to him [...] We never incited anyone to harm themselves or to end their lives instead of facing the facts before the authorities.[17]

This statement generated a dispute within public opinion about the consequences of anonymous accusations through #MeToo. There were those who blamed the movement for pushing Vega-Gil to suicide, while others argued that the act evidenced his guilt. Some argued that any expression of #Metoo ended up becoming a mechanism for blackmail, harassment, and revenge against public figures, thus tainting its claim to bring justice to victims of harassment. Others pointed out that #Metoo needed to improve its operation because of the likelihood of more accusations. Thus, a dispute was structured in which a mechanism was defended and criticized in terms of civil discourse that sought to operate as an instrument to repair the damage caused to women as victims of harassment.

---

[13] Ibid.

[14] Milenio Digital (2019, March 1).

[15] Redacción (2019, April 2).

[16] Ibid.

[17] Editor (April 3, 2019).

4.3 Smearing *#Metoo*

After Vega-Gil's suicide, three competing discourses were deployed within public opinion to signify the artist's death, as well as the purity and impurity of #Metoo. One of them accused Gil-Vega of taking his own life with the aim of discrediting the movement. From all the newspapers we sampled, *Milenio, Reforma, El Universal, Excélsior* and *La Jornada*, there were voices that stated #Metoo should not let up in its support for the victims of machismo (Albarrán, 2019; Lamas, 2019; Alanís, 2019b; El Universal, 2019; Rojas, 2019; Sefcovich, 2019; Tello, 2019; Buendía, 2019; Zuckermann, 2019). According to this view, it was important to support the movement unconditionally, as it allowed women to anonymously denounce their aggressors. It was stated that the aggressors would have to defend themselves and if they were found guilty, they would have to pay (Becerra-Acosta, 2019; Loaeza, 2019; Alanís, 2019b; Guarneros, 2019). It was certainly admitted that perhaps some women, very few, it was emphasized, could defame certain men, but that was considered a lesser evil if that would put an end to machismo (Becerra-Acosta, 2019). #Metoo had achieved, according to this interpretation, a scenario in which men would think better before harassing or raping a woman (Rojas, 2019; Guarneros, 2019). With the death of Vega-Gil, they wanted to discredit an authentic movement of thousands of women who had suffered harassment, diverting attention to the supposedly perverse character of anonymous denunciation, when such denunciation was the resource left to women wanting to make themselves heard. From this position, it was considered necessary to tell the country that #Metoo was not to blame for the death of the musician (Sierra, 2019b).

A second discourse, expressed in *Milenio, Reforma, El Universal, Excélsior*, and *La Jornada*, valued #Metoo as a legitimate movement unfortunately contaminated by fanatic activists who sought to polarize society (Revueltas, 2019). According to this discourse, the denunciations on Twitter were co-opted by political actors who believed that part of the country is comprised of people who embody goodness and the other part by subjects who embody evil. The former were considered perfect and pure, while the latter were eternally malevolent (Revueltas, 2019; Malvido, 2019). This type of stance reflected a fanaticism that turns liberating movements into oppressors, as had occurred with #Metoo. These movements did not seek justice, but rather the punishment of anyone suspected of having done something in the past, even if the events occurred decades ago (Revueltas, 2019; Clariond, 2019b). In this sense, the discourse, focused on the revenge and hatred of some #Metoo feminists, prefigured the future of a suffocating society, subjected to rancor and permanent suspicion (Revueltas, 2019: Lavín, 2019; Peñaloza, 2019b). From this perspective, it was opined that a future devoid of justice would come if those who denounced from a position of anonymity celebrated Vega-Gil's suicide (Musacchio, 2019a; Petrich, 2019; Villeda, 2019).

A third discourse directly blamed *#Metoo* for provoking the suicide of the musician. It was present in *Milenio, Reforma, El Universal, Excélsior*, and *La Jornada*, implying that the spirit and strategy that had shaped the movement aimed at accusing and judging without sufficient evidence. It was said that #Metoo put men in a situation in which they could not express their opinion or defend themselves. From this position, it was also implied that this situation was understandable, considering the damage they had caused women. But this situation had also resulted in a passive attitude that at no time questioned the credibility of women when they accused men. Thus, men could endure stoning and lynching, forbidden to defend themselves and, of course, no one would defend them because they may end up in the dock, it was said (Clariond, 2019a).

Certain journalists argued that the effects of such an accusation were devastating, because they canceled the right to advocate for innocence, having to give up public life and work. From this interpretation, anonymous accusations made harassment visible but could hurt the reputation of innocent people (García, 2019), as had occurred to Vega-Gil (Gamés, 2019a; Sarmiento, 2019). Within this positioning against #Metoo, the suicide of the musician showed that the fight against harassment was transformed into harassment against men overall: it allowed us to see that accusations—true or false—can end the life of a person who decides to sacrifice himself in desperation for not being able to defend himself (Lavín, 2019; Peñaloza, 2019b).

The argument of this discursive stance—as a normative referent of civil society discourse—is that accusations without evidence end up in lynchings, summary judgments, and moralizing slogans about the sexual behavior of men and women (Gamés, 2019b; Zamarrón, 2019a, 2019b; Buendía, 2019; Peñaloza, 2019b). Some journalists made reference to the French movement *Autre Parole*, to affirm that neither gallantry, nor insistent or clumsy seduction, is a crime (Gamés, 2019c; Musacchio, 2019b). It was claimed that Vega-Gil's suicide ended up placing so many lives out in the open—much like the victims of harassment—and hurting many more, including the musician's family– (Buendía, 2019; Malvido, 2019). From this position, it was considered necessary to distance ourselves from dichotomous visions that situated women as victims and men as victimizers (Malvido, 2019).

It was warned that Vega-Gil's suicide could not be considered a mere accident attributed to his emotional condition. According to this discourse against #Metoo, concentrated in the newspapers *Milenio* and *El Universal*, located at the center of the political spectrum and *La Jornada* on the left, there existed a real risk that anonymous denunciations could end up pushing a man to take his own life without the denouncers assuming any degree of responsibility (even if the musician had emphasized that #Metoo was not to blame for his decision) (Rocha, 2019; Peñaloza, 2019b). From this position, it was assumed that #Metoo did not stop its accusations when Vega-Gil wrote in the networks that he was going to commit suicide. From this opinion, that was the moment for #Metoo to call for reflection and say that no one is accusing anyone, that there are victims on all sides, period (Petrich, 2019). The reaction of #Metoo was described as cowardly and dastardly, with claims that the musician wanted to play with his suicide to save himself from a lawsuit for pederasty and sanitize his image. According to some commentators, the Mexican #Metoo decided to sink in its own mistakes (Petrich, 2019; Villeda, 2019).

Other voices within public opinion, emanating from *Milenio, Reforma, El Universal, Excélsior,* and *La Jornada,* pointed out that the #MeToo movement had made visible a series of tensions in Mexican society. The denunciations and the death of the musician showed the two-sided personality of the world of arts and academia, with a progressive discourse that hides its misogyny. It was also opined that the movement brought to light the two-sided personality of feminists: one that demands justice and reparation for the damage, another that is driven by hatred (Villeda, 2019). In the same vein, some cited the failure of the rule of law, because the inefficiency of the state pushed women to denounce anonymously and was unable to guarantee the presumption of innocence of the accused (Alanís, 2019a; Villanueva, 2019; Zuckermann, 2019; Peñaloza, 2019b; Poniatowska, 2019). For others, #Metoo evidenced the high degree of conservatism, machismo, and patriarchal practices that populate the relationships between men and women in Mexico (Zamarrón, 2019b; Clariond, 2019a; Lamas, 2019; Sierra, 2019a).

Some interpretations, particularly coming from *Milenio,* concluded that #Metoo could only survive if it continued to make harassment visible, but it would have to assume that justice is only possible without revenge (Villeda, 2019). Likewise, it was affirmed, from *Milenio, Excélsior* and *La Jornada,* from the center, right, and left of the political spectrum, respectively, that Vega-Gil's death should serve to improve *#Metoo* and not to silence it (Monreal, 2019; Sierra, 2019a; Virrueta, 2019; Peñaloza, 2019b). There was agreement within public opinion expressed in *Milenio, Reforma, El Universal, Excélsior,* and *La Jornada* on the need to address the causes of harassment so that the movement would not become an inquisition for men or a means to victimize women again and again—canceling their right to anonymous denunciation (Monreal, 2019; Sierra, 2019a; Virrueta, 2019; Peñaloza, 2019b). It was also considered necessary to build a broad and robust gender equity agenda that involves men (Clariond, 2019b; Sierra, 2019a), an agenda that would allow one to distinguish what is harassment from what is not: for example, is a look or a few words harassment? (Lamas, 2019). From this positioning, it was emphasized that failure to clearly differentiate this point could give way to a puritanical narrative dangerous to freedoms in all senses, not only in the field of relations between the two sexes (Lamas, 2019; Lavín, 2019).

Several writers, from *Milenio, El Universal, Excélsior,* and *La Jornada,* concluded that harassment is a serious problem in the country; accordingly, other waves of #MeToo were to be expected. They called for improving digital education in social networks (especially Twitter) to avoid the misrepresentation of comments that end up polarizing public debate (Guarneros, 2019). According to this view, Vega-Gil's death should represent an opportunity to improve the way in which messages are transmitted through social networks (Cueva, 2019; Zamarrón, 2019b). It was suggested that the movement should continue to denounce harassment without generating hate campaigns that unfairly criminalize alleged victimizers (Gamés, 2019a). From this position, the implementation of protocols to help avoid false denunciations was suggested (Rojas, 2019; Sierra, 2019a). It was recommended to implement an institutional device controlled by the state to guarantee, at the same time, the anonymity of the victim and the presumption of innocence of the accused

(Lavín, 2019; Rojas, 2019; Buendía, 2019; Virrueta, 2019), for example, through ex officio investigation of harassment complaints and determining the responsibility (or not) of the accused (Tello, 2019).

4.4 Heroes and Villains

The competition for the control of the meaning of *#Metoo* and Vega-Gil's death was articulated from three positions. Those who supported denunciation through *#Metoo*, evident in all the analyzed newspapers, considered that the movement's most relevant contribution was to give voice to the voiceless, guaranteeing anonymity, and avoiding revictimization. This position valued the testimony of the victims over the evidence. In this sense, the social punishment of the alleged harassers was more important than justice in the courts. The discrediting of the accused and of the institutions that apparently had protected them represented the path toward civil reparations for the damage suffered by women. The discrediting operates as a form of horizontal justice that highlights the verticality, normativity, and heteropatriarchal functioning of the justice system. They were, therefore, heroes who fought against heteropatriarchy. Thus, *#Metoo* was considered a civil mobilization, characterized by its rationality, realism, autonomy, and honesty, capable of generating open, critical, and frank links, and which promoted the expansion of bonds of solidarity and citizen inclusion. It also appealed to repair the damage produced by anti-civil social norms—irrational, deferential, and opaque—that normalized machismo, veiled sexual innuendo, and coercion.

Those who criticized the movement, albeit justifying its demands, warned that it had been contaminated by anti-civil actors. It was voices coming out of center and left-wing newspapers in particular, who pointed out that the misrepresentation of the civil spirit of the movement had occurred when it began to positively value revenge and social and moral sanction over law enforcement and judicial reparation of the damage. From this critical positioning, the women behind #Metoo were motivated by their feelings or passions and the claim to thoroughly modify the structures and institutions of justice. This positioning valued the movement's disdain for the legal framework as counterproductive, because it denied the presumption of innocence and due process of the accused, propitiating their media lynching. Critics of #Metoo charged that it transited from claiming civil redress to digital harassment against alleged harassers. Women could consciously or unconsciously become villains, rather than heroes.

Finally, a third position present in all newspapers except for *Reforma*, attributed anti-civil origins to #MeToo, alleging that the denunciations through Twitter assumed the presumption of guilt over the presumption of innocence. In this view, although the justice system and its functioning revictimizes women, no one could be accused only through testimonies, without providing evidence or without the version of the accused. This position questioned the fact that #Metoo put social sanction ahead of legal sanction, when it was necessary to guarantee judicial mechanisms that protected the rights of victims *and* the accused. According to this line of discourse, these regulatory procedures of legal order were the only ones that could allow for the reparation of the damage to the victims of harassment. The media mob that triggered the harassment complaints did not contribute –according to this interpretation– to the consolidation of a society based on laws and institutions.

Tables 4.1 and 4.2 show the structures of the competing discourses that marked the dispute within public opinion over *#Metoo* and the death of Vega-Gil. One can appreciate how the attributions regarding the civil character of the *#Metoo* replicate in some respects those found in the *#Metoo* and *Autre Parole* debate (see Table 3.1, Chap. 3): including the importance of status, the relationship that men and women establish (asymmetrical), the definition of harassment as domination, the importance of public denunciation, and the irrelevance of the presumption of innocence of harassers. However, one more emerges here: considering women who denounce as heroes and the relevance of the social sanctions that harassers should receive. In contrast, the anti-civil attributions to *#Metoo* replicate to some extent the impure components of the civil discourse. It is claimed that *#Metoo* only sought to satisfy selfish and particularistic interests, emphasizing that they always see relations between men and women as asymmetrical, when they are not necessarily so. Therefore, women are considered villains, moved by their emotions, who only seek revenge; in seduction relations, they always see a mechanism of domination, and complaints are made without regard to legal frameworks and without giving the opportunity to consider the presumption of innocence of those who have allegedly harassed them. These binary relationships allow us to appreciate two narrative structures within the debate and help us to understand the field of opportunity and the difficulties that exist to establish discourses and narratives that allow us to interweave the competing positions.

The suicide of Vega-Gil had generated a withdrawal of public opinion from *#Metoo* in the media, although denunciations did not stop appearing under that hashtag. All in all, the movement lost its strength significantly. However, everything changed when President López Obrador appointed an academic and an ideologue as ambassador to Panama in 2022. *#Metoo* engaged in a direct struggle with presidential power, when it pointed out that the newly appointed ambassador had been

Table 4.1 Civil classification system attributed to *#Metoo*

	Class/ Status	Female to male ratio	Women	Sanction	Harassment	Complaint	Presumption of innocence
Civil purity values	Position of power	Asymmetric	Heroes	Social	Domination	Public	No
Civil impurity values	Submission position	Symmetrical	Victims	Private	Seduction	Legal	Yes

Source: Own elaboration

Table 4.2 Anti-civil classification system attributed to *#Metoo*

	Class/Status	Female to male ratio	Women	Sanction	Harassment	Complaint	Presumption of innocence
Civil impurity values	Interests individuals	Asymmetric	Villains/irrational/ passionate	Revenge	Domination	Public	No
Civil purity values	Interests collectives	Symmetrical	Heroes/ rational	Justice	Seduction	Legal	Yes

Source: Own elaboration

accused of harassment in an institution of higher education in Mexico City. The denunciation made by *#Metoo* then confronted the populist discourse of the president, who pointed out that behind the questioning of his appointment, in reality, were the conservative and reactionary forces of the country.

4.5   *#Metoo Vis-a-Vis* Presidential Power

During his political career before becoming president, López Obrador activated a discourse characterized by a binary rhetoric that depicted a polarized society in which supposed forces of good and evil confront each other within the framework of contaminated democratic institutions (Arteaga, 2024). For López Obrador, on one side were the exploited and dominated people and, on the other, an oppressive and corrupt group, "the mafia of power," consisting of political parties, technocrats, businessmen, intellectuals, civil society, and the media. When he became president, López Obrador emphasized the need to dismantle democratic institutions, considering them instruments of the elites (Arteaga, 2021). Thus, during the first half of his six-year term, López Obrador strengthened the binary codes that sought to essentialize the behavior of political groups and actors.

As president, he assumed that he and his Fourth Transformation (4T) project were liberal, morally pure, people-centered, which privileged austerity and sought the transformation of the country. He accused his opponents of being conservative, morally impure, elitists that privileged wastefulness and that sought to sustain the status quo based on a modernization alien to the supposed traditional values of society. In contrast, López Obrador's opponents activated binary codes that allowed them to portray themselves as defenders of democracy and citizens' rights, in order to present as transparent and critical. They accused the president and his allies of being autocrats, of promoting political clienteles, while demanding deference to presidential power and the cult of López Obrador's personality.

In his inauguration as president, López Obrador stated: "We have the popular support; the people send through me to carry out the fourth transformation of the country" (Redacción AN, 2018). From that moment on, he promoted changes in the education and health systems, as well as among institutions supporting women and children under the argument that they operated as mechanisms that allowed corruption and the reproduction of power groups alien to the interests of society. When the media criticized him, the president accused them of being manipulated by power elites, economic groups, national or foreign, who wanted to reestablish the privileges they had lost with the 4T.

In a very similar tone, the president pointed out to the public that civil society organizations were mechanisms for diverting national or foreign government funding toward their benefit and interests. Feminists, human rights defenders, and academics operated, according to the president, based on a neoliberal ideological agenda that sought to perpetuate the domination of the ruling classes. According to López Obrador, these groups felt power slipping from their hands after they lost the elections, so they were constantly trying to stage a soft coup d'état against his government. Even the autonomous entities in charge of regulating the functioning of the economy or elections obstructed the consolidation of his vision for democracy in the country.

For their part, the opposition to the president's power insisted throughout his administration that he was eroding, with his speeches and actions, the institutions dedicated to addressing violence against women, education issues, and health concerns. Some media outlets argued that the president's words were a form of censorship over their work. Civil society organizations protested the closure of their funding sources. Feminists accused the president and the 4T of being sexist and misogynist. In sum, the opposition accused López Obrador of authoritarianism, of strengthening his political clientele rather than citizen practices, and demanding deference to him from the media and political groups. Both positions depicted a polarized country that expressed a kind of moral agonism confronting social forces that embodied good and evil. Each protagonist presented those he considered his allies as honest, democratic, autonomous, and authentic, accusing the others of being dishonest and anti-democratic. The competing actors interpreted every action or speech of their opponents as proof of perversion and moral decay.

In this context, the President appointed historian Pedro Salmerón as Mexico's ambassador to Panama in 2022. The announcement brought to light the alleged acts of harassment of female students at the Instituto Tecnológico Autónomo de México (ITAM). The student organization, the Fourth Wave, rejected Salmerón's appointment and launched the #UnAcosadorNoDebeSerEmbajador (Fourth Wave, 2022). The organization called on the president to reconsider the appointment and obtain justice for the women Salmerón had harassed. The Observatorio Mexicano de Política Exterior Feminista warned that the appointment did not guarantee a Secretary of Foreign Affairs free of violence against women (Observatorio Mexicano de Política Exterior Feminista, 2022). These remarks sought to warn of the supposedly contaminated character that Salmerón's person carried, and that could infect the office to which he was appointed.

The president defended Salmerón. He pointed out that he was a capable person, one of the best historians in the country, and reassured the public that there were no criminal charges against him. He denied that the complaints about the historian at ITAM, which had to do with the positions of conservatism, could serve as a pretext for the Panamanian government to reject his proposed ambassador. The president maintained that he did not intend to reconsider his appointment only because of the media lynching to which he was subjected in social networks and in the newspaper *Reforma* (Redacción AN, 2022). In fact, he considered Salmerón to embody civil virtue: a reasonable man, not subject to his passions, who sustained open relationships and who could strengthen the institutions of the state. The greatest presidential power wielded by López Obrador was that there was no legal proof against Salmerón. On the contrary, those who pointed to Salmerón as a harasser carried the components of civil vice: groups mobilized by their selfish and particularistic interests, who operated out of the public eye and who wanted institutions to remain the hostages of a few.

The voices in public opinion—coming from the liberal left newspapers *Reforma* and *La Jornada*, which supported Salmerón's appointment as ambassador, pointed out that there were different versions of the alleged harassment allegations against him, so it was unclear whether he was guilty or a victim of defamation (Gershenson, 2022). It was argued that the president had adequately defended Salmerón (Hernández, 2022a) and it was lamented that the appointment put the historian in the public eye to revive the non-judicial accusations against him (Hernández, 2022b). Thus, those who defended Salmerón's appointment interpreted the designation as recognition of a great historian who had been unfairly accused by the conservative right. In the end, the argument for presidential power was replicated within public opinion, echoing that Salmerón was an academic and that he had no legal accusations against him.

As shown in Table 4.3, the president had tried to contaminate the #Metoo movement using class references, namely, that the mobilized women responded to particularistic interests from which they even received funding, as well as its alleged political link with what he considered conservatism. Likewise, López Obrador sought to contaminate the movement by emphasizing that it only sought the public denunciation and lynching of Salmerón, and that they did not care about the presumption of innocence. However, the most important thing as a mechanism of significance to consider the purity or impurity of the *#Metoo* demands, according to López Obrador, was whether or not they had a relationship with presidential power. This last assignment, regarding the relationship of feminists to the power of a president, was an innovation in the contamination system reproduced within public opinion. Feminists tried to point out that López Obrador was distancing himself from the function of the office of president by assuming that he was the representative of the universe of feminists in the country. In other words, he was emptying the office of its function as a universalist understanding of the organization of the country's authority.

For their part, critics of Salmerón's appointment, concentrated in the right–wing daily *Excélsior*, the centrists *Milenio* and *El Universal*, as well as the liberal daily *Reforma*, claimed that the president was trying to benefit the historian as ambassador because he was part of the most radical group within MORENA and a friend of the president's wife (Soto, 2022; Bartolomé, 2022a). It was warned that the

Table 4.3 Rating system attributed to *#Metoo* by presidential power

	Class/ Status	Women	Complaint	Sanction	Presumption of innocence	Relationship with presidential power
Anti- civil values	Particular interests	Conservatives	Public	Lynching	No	No
Civil values	People's interests	Progressives	Legal	Justice	Yes	Yes

Source: Own elaboration

protection Salmerón received from the ruling group would go against the group of feminists of his party, who pointed to him as a harasser (Zárate, 2022). López Obrador, it was said, defended Salmerón because he was a great historian (Arvizu, 2022), but in reality, he was an "officialism historian" (Márquez, 2022), "in the pay of the regime" (Catón, 2022). He was a bad historian (Gamés, 2022) who promoted a Manichean vision of history, in which liberals and revolutionaries possess all the civil virtues, while conservatives possess all the civil vices (Gutiérrez, 2022). In this way, critical voices tried to place Salmerón at the opposite pole of the system of signification of civil discourse from which the president had placed him. He was, according to this view, a person who bore anti-civil attributes: a bad academic who would become an ambassador by being part of a power group, driven by selfishness, who reproduces relationships based on personal interest and oriented to the conspiracy headed by a president that fosters personal relationships.

The criticism went further, from all newspapers, except the leftist *La Jornada*, accusing López Obrador of being indignant because the accusations against Salmerón lacked formal basis, while the president himself judged every day without evidence those he considers his political enemies (Pérez, 2022a; Jáuregui, 2022, Bartolomé, 2022b; Murillo, 2022; Sierra, 2022; Soto, 2022). Critics argued that the president ignored the difficulty a woman faces in filing a harassment complaint, the "ordeal of revictimization" and "not being believed" (Dresser, 2022). The president had "lamentably" defended an alleged harasser, damaging the dignity of the government (Garfias, 2022). The saddest thing, it was said, is that feminists of his party had supported the position of the Mexican president in social networks (Martínez, 2022).

The appointment of the historian as ambassador was to be interpreted, according to this position, as a humiliating act that minimized the strength of the feminist movement (Manzo, 2022; Sarmiento, 2022). De la Barreda (2022), the appointment of Salmerón was an act through which women were told "that the unconditional supporters of the government tolerate any affront against them, that the unconditional support of the aggressor outweighs respect for them." If his status as ambassador to Panama were to be ratified, it was likely that he would be marginalized by the Panamanian government (Lomónaco, 2022). However, it was assured, the president would not overturn his appointment because he believed that such an action would strengthen his critics (Zepeda, 2022) and the feminist movement, which he considered conservative; it would further be useful for the enemies of the transformation he claimed to lead (De la Barreda, 2022).

Given the scenario of competition for the direction of Salmerón's appointment as ambassador, the Panamanian Foreign Minister, Erika Mouynes, announced that she had established through diplomatic means the position of her country with respect to the appointment (Telemetro Reporta, 2022). Meanwhile, more than 100 feminist organizations from Mexico and Panama asked the president of Panama not to approve Salmerón (Redacción AN, 2022). At the beginning of February, the president of Mexico announced that the Panamanian Foreign Ministry had rejected the proposal. He regretted that Foreign Minister Mouynes had become Salmerón's judge and that she had been guided by a scandal of alleged harassment at ITAM, saying that "it turns out that we proposed him [Salmerón] for ambassador to

Panama –argued the president– and, as if it were the Holy Inquisition, the Panamanian minister or foreign minister disagreed, because they were in disagreement at ITAM" (Martínez & Cruz, 2022).

López Obrador affirmed that surely the Panamanian president was not even aware of Mouynes' decision. The Mexican president then released a letter from Salmerón in which the historian announced that he was "stepping aside" from his nomination to avoid turning his appointment into an issue of gender and international politics, attesting that the policy of the current government "has made the historical demands of the feminist movement a reality" (La Silla Rota, 2022). López Obrador announced that he would appoint another person as ambassador, the actor Jesusa Rodríguez, and pointed out that he hoped that this new appointment would not upset the conservative right (Martínez & Cruz, 2022). Thus, in the face of the rejection of his ambassadorial proposal, López Obrador equated the position of the Panamanian foreign minister with what he attributed to the opposition in Mexico: conservative, feminist, and intransigent towards authority, because she apparently had not informed the (male) president about the appointment of Salmerón.

Before the accusations toward Foreign Minister Mouynes, the Panamanian diplomacy had communicated: "We have no official comment" (Meléndez, 2022). However, the former president of Panama, Ernesto Pérez Balladares, asserted that the reaction of the Mexican president was childish, adding "[W]e are a small but dignified and brave country. Mexico needs us more than we need Mexico" (Pérez, 2022b). Thus, he situated Mexico's president as an irrational, hysterical, easily excitable actor, who had, like any infant, a distorted view of reality. Likewise, public opinion in Panama accused López Obrador of being petulant and arrogant in the way he treated the foreign minister; he embodied characteristics considered contaminants in civil discourse. A Panamanian journalist affirmed that the Mexican president was a "textbook macho man," who denigrated women by saying that Foreign Minister Mouynes had decided without the endorsement of the president of Panama, as if "executive-political women could not make a decision with arguments… and it was a burst of madness... it is the typical macho argumentation" (Barragán, 2022).

4.6   The Polarized Structure of Meaning

In this chapter, we have shown how complaints from the public about harassment. as a structure of feelings of democratic life, have made it possible to expose people who had exercised their position of power over women in different spaces. The purpose of these denunciations was not only to make visible the moments in which women are placed in a situation of physical vulnerability, but also to generate support for a dynamic of solidarity, civil reparation, and expansion of the mechanisms for the social inclusion of women. However, a debate was generated in which, from one side, the testimony of women who claimed to have been harassed was seen as more important than concrete evidence, and, on the other, those who made the complaints were moved by revenge and emotions and not by claims of justice, reparation, and moderation. Moreover, one could ask, how could one defend the presumption of innocence, evidence, and institutions when the justice system revictimizes women to such an extent that it operates against the reparation of damages in the face of harassment? Each of these positions called for broad forms of solidarity and social inclusion. However, each position attributed to its counterparts the supposed defense of particularistic and exclusionary positions of solidarity and inclusion.

The classification system of *#Metoo* was activated again in the controversy triggered when the movement was confronted with presidential power, when the president had rejected the civil character of the mobilization against the individual he had appointed as ambassador to Panama. Feminist critics warned that the president sought to delegitimize a legitimate demand. The confrontation in relation to Salmerón's statements and his appointment as ambassador to Panama was articulated in terms of the structure of political meaning in which the competing sides imputed attributes of civil impurity to each other. In this way, a moral agonism was generated; the historian served as a horizon of meaning through which both camps sought to eliminate each other as valid (civil) interlocutors. Arguments about a possible alternative interpretation of history or about the meaning of harassment and the ways to establish responsibilities for it were diluted to unveil the morally valid or invalid attributes of those who speak or act, of those who considered themselves victims and victimizers of some act of violence. This type of typification is not new for democracy, which operates by assigning civil or anti-civil attributes to its members.

What the two arenas of dispute around Salmerón have shown is the degree to which the typification essentializes those involved in the political debate within public opinion, assigning them attributes with which they suppress each other as legitimate interlocutors. This process contributes to eroding the construction of a vital democratic center. Each camp is unable to recognize each other positively in moral and emotional terms, but perhaps more importantly, they dilute the possibility of opening a space for dialogue to discuss the meanings of harassment and violence in the country beyond political and ideological differences. When any discussion is articulated in this polarized structure of meaning—such as those presented in relation to Salmerón—it becomes difficult for members of a civil community to treat and reason with each other as they accuse each other of being contaminated.

References

Alanís, E. (2019a, April 5). AMLO prevailed, 'however it happened, however it happened'. *El Universal.* https://www.eluniversal.com.mx/columna/elisa-alanis/nacion/amlo-se-impuso-haiga-sido-como-haiga-sido

Alanís, M. (2019b, April 12). #MeToo and access to justice. *El Universal.* https://www.eluniversal.com.mx/articulo/maria-del-carmen-alanis/nacion/metoo-y-el-acceso-la-justicia

Albarrán, J. (2019, April 5). What is safe is no longer a mystery. *Milenio.*. https://www.milenio. com/opinion/jairo-calixto-albarran/politica-cero/lo-seguro-ya-no-tiene-misterio

AP Agency. (2017, November 28). Women comedians in Mexico warn about gender violence in their industry. *El Comercio.* https://www.elcomercio.com/tendencias/mujeres-comediantes-mexico-violenciadegenero-industria.html

Arteaga, N. (2021). The populist transition and the civil sphere in Mexico. In J. Alexander, G. Sciortino, & P. Kivisto (Eds.), *Populism in the civil sphere* (pp. 96–124). Polity Press.

Arteaga, N. (2024). *The civil sphere and the semantics of political dispute.* FLACSO Mexico.

Arvizu, E. (2022, January 30). Not so much that it burns the saint. *El Universal.* https://www. eluniversal.com.mx/opinion/eduardo-arvizu/ni-tanto-que-queme-al-santo/

Avila, Y. (2019, March 27). How did the Me Too movement emerge and how did it revive in Mexico. *Animal Político.* https://animalpolitico.com/verificacion-de-hechos/te-explico/como-surgio-el-movimiento-me-too-y-como-revivio-en-mexico

Barragán, S. (2022, February 2). Strong criticism of AMLO from politicians in Panama: childish, arrogant and arrogant. *Aristegui Noticias.* https://aristeguinoticias.com/0202/mexico/fuertes-criticas-de-politicos-de-panama-a-amlo-infantil-prepotente-y-soberbio/

Bartolomé, F. (2022a, January 18). Templo Mayor. *Reforma.* https://www.reforma.com/templo-mayor-f-bartolome-2023-01-18/op241779

Bartolomé, F. (2022b, January 20). Templo Mayor *Reforma.* https://www.reforma.com/templo-mayor-f-bartolome-2022-01-20/op219740

Becerra-Acosta, J. (2019, August 19). Angry women… and unpunished males. *Milenio.* https://www.milenio.com/opinion/juan-pablo-becerra-acosta/doble-fondo/mujeres-furiosas-y-machos-impunes

Buendía, J. (2019, April 7). #MeToo Mexico: Will it continue? *Excélsior.* https://www.excelsior.com.mx/opinion/jose-buendia-hegewisch/metoo-mexico-continuara/1306247

Catón. (2022, February 3). Bad... and worse! *Reforma.* https://busquedas.gruporeforma.com/reforma/Documento/Web.aspx?id=216124|Opinion&url=https://www.gruporeforma.com/Opinion/Autor/442_perfilArtOCNRM.jpg&text=Pedro+Salmer%f3n&tit=

Clariond, A. (2019a, April 3). Complaining is prohibited. *Reforma.* https://www.reforma.com/prohibido-quejarse-2019-04-03/op153899

Clariond, A. (2019b, October 2). This is not a protest. *Reforma.* https://www.gruporeforma.com/Opinion/Autor/771_perfilArtOCNRM.jpg&text=Pedro+Salmer%f3n&tit=

Cueva, Á. (2019, April 7). Death and #MeToo. *Milenio.* https://www.milenio.com/opinion/alvaro-cueva/ojo-por-ojo/la-muerte-y-metoo

De la Barreda, L. (2022, February 3). A historic achievement. *Excélsior.* https://www.excelsior.com.mx/opinion/luis-de-la-barreda-solorzano/un-logro-historico/1496493

Dresser, D. (2022, January 31). Halo of hypocrisy. *Reforma.* https://www.gruporeforma.com/Opinion/Autor/463_perfilArtOCNRM.jpg&text=Pedro+Salmer%f3n&tit=

Editor. (2019, April 3). #MeTooMúsicosMexicos suspends its activity on Twitter. *Estados del Tiempo.* https://estadodeltiempo.mx/metoomusicosmexicos-desaparece-de-Twitter/

El Universal. (2019, April 10). Harassment: is it useful to report? El Universal. https://www.eluniversal.com.mx/articulo/editorial-el-universal/nacion/acoso-sirve-denunciar

Fourth Wave [@FourthWave] (2022, January 17). #AHarasserMustNotBeAmbassador. *Twitter.*

Frías, S. (2019). Harassment and sexual harassment. The case of a law enforcement institution. *Estudios Sociológicos de El Colegio de México, 38*(112), 103–139. https://doi.org/10.24201/en.2020v38n112.1745

Fuentes, A. (2019, March 31). More than a hashtag, a cry of despair. *El Universal.* https://www.eluniversal.com.mx/articulo/angelica-fuentes/cartera/mas-que-un-hashtag-un-grito-de-desesperacion

Fundar Centro de Análisis. (2017). *Contra la violencia que no se ve.* https://fundar.org.mx/contra-la-violencia-que-no-se-ve/

Gamés, G. (2019a, September 23). The quality of the marshmallow. *Milenio.* https://www.milenio.com/opinion/gil-games/uno-hasta-el-fondo/la-calidad-de-la-melcocha_2

Gamés, G. (2019b, September 24). The brave do murder. *Milenio*. https://www.milenio.com/opinion/gil-games/uno-hasta-el-fondo/los-valientes-si-asesinan

Gamés, G. (2019c, April 8). Capture and submit. *Milenio*. https://www.milenio.com/opinion/gil-games/uno-hasta-el-fondo/capturar-y-someter

Gamés, G. (2022, January 26). There goes the water and it smells like gas. *Milenio*. https://www.milenio.com/opinion/gil-games/uno-hasta-el-fondo/ahi-va-el-agua-y-huele-a-gas

García, S. (2019, August 20). AMLO's "happy, happy" people. *El Universal*. https://www.eluniversal.com.mx/opinion/salvador-garcia-soto/el-pueblo-feliz-feliz-de-amlo

Garfias, F. (2022, February 23). Tension between Mexico and Panama. *Excélsior*. https://www.excelsior.com.mx/opinion/francisco-garfias/tension-entre-mexico-y-panama/1496480

Gershenson, C. (2022, February 1). Impunity. *Reforma*. https://www.reforma.com/impunidad-2022-02-01/op220478

Guarneros, F. (2019, March 31). #MeToo. *Excélsior*. https://www.excelsior.com.mx/opinion/fabiola-guarneros-saavedra/metoo/1304864

Gutiérrez, A. (2022, February 3). Mexico stumbles against Panama. *Milenio*. https://www.milenio.com/opinion/agustin-gutierrez-canet/sin-ataduras/tropieza-mexico-con-panama

Hernández, J. (2022a, January 19). Astillero. La *Jornada*. https://www.jornada.com.mx/2022/01/19/opinion/010o1pol

Hernández, J. (2022b, January 26). Astillero. *La Jornada*. https://www.jornada.com.mx/2022/01/26/opinion/008o1pol%20(26

Instituto Nacional de las Mujeres (INMUJERES). (2017). *Informe estadístico de registro de casos de hostigamiento sexual y acoso sexual en la administración pública federal (Statistical report on the registration of cases of sexual harassment and sexual harassment in the federal public administration)*. https://www.gob.mx/cms/uploads/attachment/file/403545/Informe_Casos_Hostigamiento.pdf

Instituto Nacional de las Mujeres (INMUJERES), Secretaría de la Función Pública (SFP) & Comisión Nacional para prevenir y Erradicar la Violencia Contra las Mujeres (CONAVIM). (2018). *Informe estadístico de registro de casos de hostigamiento sexual y acoso sexual en la administración pública Federal 2018*. https://www.gob.mx/cms/uploads/attachment/file/506540/Informe_General_de_Casos_VF.pdf

Jáuregui, M. (2022, January 19). Protector. *Reforma*. https://www.gruporeforma.com/Opinion/generica.jpg&text=Pedro+Salmer%f3n&tit=

La Silla Rota. (2022, February 1). CPM Letter from Pedro Salmerón, 01feb22. *Scribd*. https://es.scribd.com/document/556307909/CPM-Carta-de-Pedro-Salmeron-01feb22#download&from_embed

Lamas, M. (2019, April 5). Dilemmas about bullying. *Reforma*. https://www.reforma.com/aplicaciones/editoriales/editorial.aspx?id=154071

Lavín, M. (2019, April 13). Questions and jacarandas. *El Universal*. https://www.eluniversal.com.mx/columna/monica-lavin/cultura/preguntas-y-jacarandas

Loaeza, G. (2019, April 9). #MeToo. *Reforma*. https://www.reforma.com/aplicaciones/editoriales/editorial.aspx?id=154285

Lomónaco, J. (2022, February 1). The 4T reached the SEM. *El Universal*.

Malvido, A. (2019, April 17). #MeToo, ethics, art and Testosterone. *El Universal*. https://www.eluniversal.com.mx/columna/adriana-malvido/cultura/metoo-etica-arte-y-testosterona

Manzo, L. (2022, January 20). Skipping all the women. *El Universal*. https://www.eluniversal.com.mx/opinion/laura-manzo/saltarse-todas-las-mujeres/

Márquez, R. (2022, January 21). Impunity for criminals. *Excélsior*. excelsior.com.mx/opinion/ricardo-alexander-marquez/impunidad-a-los-criminales/1494319%20(21

Martínez, F. & Cruz, A. (2022, February 2). Canciller de Panamá rechazó la designación de Salmerón: AMLO. *La Jornada*. https://www.jornada.com.mx/notas/2022/02/02/politica/canciller-de-panama-rechazo-la-designacion-de-salmeron-amlo/

Martínez, J. (2022, January 22). The virtues of Salmerón. *Milenio*. https://www.milenio.com/opinion/jose-luis-martinez/el-santo-oficio/las-virtudes-de-salmeron

Maza, V. (2019, March 30). Reflections on #MeToo. *Milenio*. https://www.milenio.com/opinion/veronica-maza-bustamante/el-sexodromo/reflexiones-sobre-el-metoo

McLean, J. (2020). *Changing digital geographies, changing digital geographies*. Palgrave Macmillan.

Meléndez, J. (2022, February 1). 'No comment,' says Panama's Foreign Ministry after AMLO's comments about Erika Mouynes. *El Universal*. https://www.eluniversal.com.mx/cultura/panama-sin-comentarios-dicen-en-cancilleria-tras-dichos-de-amlo-sobre-erika-mouynes/

Milenio Digital. (2019, March 1). Me Too Mexican Musicians Return to Twitter; Accuse of Censorship Attempt. *Milenio*. https://www.google.com/search?q=traductor&rlz=1C1CHBD_esMX1163MX1163&oq=tr&gs_lcrp=EgZjaHJvbWUqDggAEEUYJxg7GIAEGIoF-Mg4IABBFGCcYOxiABBiKBTIGCAEQRRhAMgYIAhBFGDkyDAgDECMYJxiABBiKBTISCAQQQABhDGIMBGLEDGIAEGIoFMgYIBRBFGD0yBggGEEUY-PDIGCAcQRRg80gEIMjQ1MWowajeoAgCwAgA&sourceid=chrome&ie=UTF-8

Monreal, C. (2019, April 8). #MeToo: neither lynching nor revictimization. *Excélsior*. https://www.excelsior.com.mx/opinion/opinion-del-experto-nacional/metoo-ni-linchamiento-ni-revictimizacion/1306381

Murillo, A. (2022, January 21). Enough. *Reforma*. https://www.gruporeforma.com/Opinion/Autor/1308_perfilArtOCNRM.jpg&text=Pedro+Salmer%f3n&tit=

Musacchio, H. (2019a September 26). The target is AMLO, not Salmerón. *Excélsior*. https://www.excelsior.com.mx/opinion/humberto-musacchio/el-objetivo-es-amlo-no-salmeron/1338470

Musacchio, H. (2019b, April 4). The harassment of Armando Vega-Gil. *Excélsior*. https://www.excelsior.com.mx/opinion/humberto-musacchio/el-acoso-a-armando-vega-gil/1305701

Nicolas-Gavilan, M. T., Baptista-Lucio, M. P., & Padilla-Lavin, M. A. (2019). Effects of the #MeToo campaign in media, social and political spheres: The case of Mexico. *Interactions: Studies in Communication & Culture, 10*(3), 273–290. https://doi.org/10.1386/iscc.10.3.273_1

Observatorio Mexicano de Política Exterior Feminista [@ompef_mx] (2022, January 17). This fact is a total incongruence with #FeministForeignPolicy, since, once again, its policy neither questions nor transforms. *Twitter*. https://x.com/ompef_mx/status/1483232112841011202

Peñaloza, P. (2019a, March 29). Sound route. La Jornada. https://www.jornada.com.mx/2019/03/29/opinion/a08o1esp

Peñaloza, P. (2019b, April 5). Ruta sonora. For a less irresponsible #MeTooMúsicosMexicanos. *La Jornada*. https://www.jornada.com.mx/2019/04/05/opinion/a10o1esp

Pérez, C. (2022a, February 1). Complaints and whistleblowers. *El Universal*. https://www.eluniversal.com.mx/opinion/catalina-perez-correa/denuncias-y-denunciantes/

Pérez, E. (2022b, February 2). Mr. López Obrador's attitude regarding the appointment of his representative in our country is childish. *Twitter*. https://x.com/PerezBalladares/status/1488870735661645824?ref_src=twsrc%5Etfw%7Ctwcamp%5Etweetembed%7Ctwterm%5E1488870735661645824%7Ctwgr%5E%7Ctwcon%5Es1_&ref_url=https%3A%2F%2Fwww.etcetera.com.mx%2Fnacional%2Freaccion-amlo-salmeron-infantil-expresidente-panama%2F

Petrich, B. (2019, April 3). The Mexican #MeToo, bonfire out of control. *La Jornada*. https://www.jornada.com.mx/2019/04/03/opinion/017a1pol

Poniatowska, E. (2019, April 4). Outrageous anonymous denunciations. *La Jornada*. https://www.jornada.com.mx/2019/04/04/opinion/a04a1esp

Redacción AN. (2018, August 8). This was AMLO's speech after receiving constancy as president-elect (Video). *Aristegui Noticias*. https://aristeguinoticias.com/0808/mexico/este-fue-el-discurso-de-amlo-tras-recibir-constancia-de-presidente-electo-video/

Redacción. (2019, April 2). Armando Vega: What is known about the accusations against the founder of Botellita de Jerez that appeared on @metoomusicamx? BBC News Mundo. https://www.bbc.com/mundo/noticias-america-latina-47786292

Redacción AN. (2020, March 8). The faces of #MeToo in Mexico: from harassment to outrage. *Aristegui Noticias*. https://aristeguinoticias.com/0803/mexico/los-rostros-del-metoo-en-mexico-del-acoso-a-la-indignacion/

Redacción AN. (2022, January 26). AMLO defends Pedro Salmerón and compares his case to that of Rosario Piedra. *Aristegui Noticias*. https://aristeguinoticias.com/2601/mexico/amlo-defiende-a-pedro-salmeron-y-compara-su-caso-con-el-de-rosario-piedra-enterate/

Revueltas, R. (2019, April 7). Confiscated feminism. Milenio. https://www.milenio.com/opinion/roman-revueltas-retes/la-semana-de-roman-revueltas-retes/el-feminismo-confiscado

Rhode, D. (2019). #METOO: WHY NOW ? WHAT NEXT ?', Duke Law Journal, 69(2), 377428.

Rivera, C. (2020). Women against the Femicide Machine in Mexico. *World Literature Today*, *94*(1), 50–54. https://doi.org/10.11693/hyhz20181000233

Rocha, R. (2019, April 3). Don't blame anyone for his death. *El Universal*. https://www.eluniversal.com.mx/articulo/ricardo-rocha/nacion/no-se-culpe-nadie-de-su-muerte

Rodríguez, L., Barraza, D., Salazar, J., & Vargas, R. (2019). Index of suicide risk in Mexico using Twitter. *Journal of Social Researches, 5*(15), 1–13. https://doi.org/10.35429/jsr.2019.15.5.1.13

Rojas, P. (2019, April 8). From secret harassment to anonymous whistleblowing. *El Universal*. https://www.eluniversal.com.mx/columna/paola-rojas/nacion/del-acoso-secreto-la-denuncia-anonima

Sánchez, M. (2020). Public policies for gender equality in Mexico. *International Journal of Human Rights, 10*(1), 175–212.

Sarmiento, S. (2019, April 2). No way out. *Reforma*. https://www.reforma.com/aplicaciones/editoriales/editorial.aspx?id=153866

Sarmiento, S. (2022, December 19). Friends ambassadors. *Reforma*. https://www.gruporeforma.com/Opinion/Autor/548_perfilArtOCNRM.jpg&text=Pedro+Salmer%f3n&tit=

Sefcovich, S. (2019, April 7). MeToo and other justice. *El Universal*. https://www.eluniversal.com.mx/articulo/sara-sefchovich/nacion/metoo-y-otras-justicias

Sierra, Y. (2019a, April 6). Shake the earth. *Excélsior.* https://www.excelsior.com.mx/opinion/yuriria-sierra/cimbrar-la-tierra/1306103

Sierra, Y. (2019b, April 2). It's not #MeToo's fault. *Excelsior.* https://www.excelsior.com.mx/opinion/yuriria-sierra/la-culpa-no-es-del-metoo/1305218

Sierra, Y. (2022, January 21). Ambassador. Excélsior. https://www.excelsior.com.mx/opinion/yuriria-sierra/embajador/1494312

Soto, C. (2022, January 23). Salmerón: the third time is the charm. *Excélsior*. https://www.excelsior.com.mx/opinion/cecilia-soto/salmeron-la-tercera-es-la-vencida/1494547

Telemetro Reporta [@TReporta] (2022, January 24). Panamanian Foreign Minister Erika Mouynes said that the Mexican Foreign Ministry was notified through diplomatic channels of the official position on the appointment of Pedro Salmerón as Mexican ambassador to Panama. *Twitter*. https://x.com/TReporta/status/1485647271752613893?ref_src=twsrc%5Etfw%7Ctwcamp%5Etweetembed%7Ctwterm%5E1485647271752613893%7Ctwgr%5E%7Ctwcon%5Es1_&ref_url=https%3A%2F%2Fwww.eluniversal.com.mx%2Fcultura%2Fpanama-ya-manifesto-mexico-su-posicion-por-designacion-de-pedro-salmeron

Tello, I. (2019, April 5). #MeToo and the shortcomings of the criminal justice system. *El Universal*. https://www.eluniversal.com.mx/articulo/irene-tello-arista/nacion/metoo-y-las-deficiencias-del-sistema-de-justicia-penal

Vega Gil, A. [@ArmandoVegaGil] (2019, April 1). No se culpe a nadie de mi muerte: es un suicidio, una decisión voluntaria, consciente, libre y personal. #MeeToMusicosMexicanos. *Twitter*. https://x.com/ArmandoVegaGil/status/1112666222951391233

Vela, E. (2019, March 31). #MeToo. *Reforma*. https://www.reforma.com/aplicaciones/editoriales/editorial.aspx?id=153730&referer=%2D%2D7d616165662f3a3a6262623b727a7a727970 3b767a783a%2D%2D

Villanueva, E. (2019, April 3). The scope of #MeToo. *Excélsior.* https://www.excelsior.com.mx/nacional/el-opinador-en-excelsior-digital-los-alcances-de-metoo/1305566

Villeda, A. (2019, April 6). #MeToo and the split personality. *Milenio*. https://www.milenio.com/opinion/alfredo-villeda/fusilerias/metoo-y-la-doble-personalidad

Virrueta, P. (2019, April 3). The responsibility of a #hashtag. *Excélsior.* https://www.excelsior.com.mx/opinion/paola-virrueta/la-responsabilidad-de-un-hashtag/1305234

Zamarrón, H. (2019a, March 31). Sex is politics, let's talk. *Milenio.* https://www.milenio.com/opinion/hector-zamarron/afinidades-selectivas/el-sexo-es-politica-hablemos

Zamarrón, H. (2019b, April 7). The new conservatism. *Milenio.* https://www.milenio.com/opinion/hector-zamarron/afinidades-selectivas/el-nuevo-conservadurismo

Zárate, A. (2022, January 19). Lost diplomacy. *El Universal.* https://www.eluniversal.com.mx/opinion/alfonso-zarate/diplomacia-extraviada%20(19/

Zepeda, J. (2022, February 3). Do we have a misogynist president? *Milenio.* https://www.milenio.com/opinion/jorge-zepeda-patterson/pensandolo-bien/tenemos-un-presidente-misogino

Zuckermann, L. (2019, April 2). On the #MeToo movement and the suicide of Armando Vega. *Excélsior.* https://www.excelsior.com.mx/opinion/leo-zuckermann/sobre-el-movimiento-metoo-y-el-suicidio-de-armando-vega/1305214

Chapter 5
If They Disappear… Destroy Everything!

Abstract This chapter explores how two opposing discourses contested the meaning of the #NoMeCiudanMeViolan mobilization and its impact on the social inclusion of women in relation to presidential power, particularly under the leadership of the Mexico City government. Characterized by violent actions, this mobilization was effective in amplifying women's voices and demanding that public opinion, as a symbolic representation of the 'public," demonstrate solidarity with their demands. Additionally, it played a crucial role in creating and solidifying a new set of semantic innovations, portraying women not only as victims but also as heroines and anti-heroines.

Keywords Feminist mobilization · Legitimate violent protests · Illegitimate violent protests · Women heroes · Women anti-heroes

5.1 The Rising Tide of Indignation

On August 16, 2019, a feminist march was held in Mexico City (CDMX) under the name #NoMeCiudanMeViolan (#NMCMV). The protestors denounced the lack of attention and response by the authorities to cases of violence against women by the capital's police. During the march, monuments were painted and graffitied, while some public services, including a Metrobus station and a police station, were destroyed. These actions were considered by the public opinion as the innovative acts of a feminist protest in Mexico. However, they unleashed a dispute about the legitimacy of such actions. The objective of this chapter is to analyze how two competing discourses disputed the meaning of the protest, as well as to unpack its effects on social inclusion for women in their relationship with presidential power through the head of the government of Mexico City. On the one hand, a discourse was

L. A. Cardona Acuña, N. Arteaga Botello, *Feminism, Power and Public Opinion in Mexico*, SpringerBriefs in Sociology,
https://doi.org/10.1007/978-3-032-14141-5_5

developed that considered the acts of protest and "vandalism" of the demonstrators as expression of their weariness and tiredness before the apathy of the authorities. In this view, violence was a civil resource to transform the public life of the city. On the other hand, a discourse was constructed that bet on judging the use of violence in the protest as inappropriate, not only because it was a mobilization trapped in emotion and irrationality, but also because it was aimed at destabilizing the local government and, consequently, presidential power.

The event that sparked the #NMCMV mobilization sought to convey and translate feelings of exclusion, indignation, and the impossibility of access to justice for what was seen as a possible dismissal of the investigation into the alleged rape of a young woman by Mexico City police officers in August 2019. This fact was signified by a group of activists as an unacceptable act. The violence unleashed during the protest was interpreted in the logic of the binary discourse of civil society as an incomprehensible and unjustifiable action, hence, an irrational, anti-civil act, as well as an understandable and justifiable act, hence, civil and reasonable, based on the motives, relationships and institutions that were put into play. The competition between these two discourses allows us to understand the disputes within public opinion about the pure and impure character of the feminist movement that sought to broaden solidarity, as well as to generate processes of civil redress in the face of violence against women.

The central argument of the chapter is that the dispute over the meaning of the #NMCMV protest put into competition two narratives, first a narrative within public opinion that sought to attribute a pure or civil character to the women who participated in it, thereby underlining its capacity to generate more universal and supportive memberships of inclusion. A second narrative tried to contaminate and point out the anti-civil profile of the mobilization, highlighting that its proposal was apparently restricted in terms of solidarity and social inclusion. To support this argument about the two competing narratives, we first outline the context prior to the #NMCMV protest, significant for those who opined about it. Subsequently, we analyze the disputes to control the meaning of the mobilization and then shed light on how the dispute over meanings emerged within the contours of a debate about what can be considered (or not) new feminist justice.

On December 1, 2018, Andrés Manuel López Obrador assumed the Mexican presidency, supported by the Morena party, and progressive social movements and organizations. Four days later, Claudia Sheinbaum (also from MORENA) became the mayor of the country's capital. She was a politician who had been very close to the president for a long time, considered one of the possible candidates to succeed him.[1]

---

[1] Sheinbaum's political life was indeed linked closely to that of López Obrador. When the latter was the head of the government for Mexico City between 2006 and 2012, Sheinbaum was his secretary of the environment. Although she returned to her academic life at the National Autonomous University of Mexico at the end of her term as secretary, she remained a militant in the Democratic Revolution Party (PRD), in which López Obrador was also a militant. When López Obrador founded MORENA, Sheinbaum followed him, later becoming mayor of Tlalapan and then the mayor of Mexico City. She is now the first female president of the Mexican republic.

The capital was a city that often appeared in the media with worrying figures on femicide and violence against women (Galván, 2019). "Missing woman found dead!" was one of the most frequent headlines in the Mexican media. Figures have shown that from 2015 to 2018 there were 3578 cases of femicide, of which 231 were in Mexico City.[2] In her inauguration as mayor on December 5, 2018, Claudia Sheinbaum acknowledged this problem (Excélsior, 2018). That day she declared that she would work "with energy to eradicate gender violence and bring justice in cases of femicide.[3]

However, from the first days of Sheinbaum's administration, there were reports of attempted kidnappings of women in the Metro Collective Transport System (Data Cívica & Torreblanca, 2019). Some media sources reported around 200 testimonies of alleged cases, as well as "27 investigations for kidnapping, 73 for illegal deprivation of liberty and 170 for abduction of minors."[4] This reportage generated a feminist mobilization on February 2, 2019 at the Monumento a la Madre, which declared that "neither the mayor nor the president of the republic had made pronouncements on the issue" (Proceso, 2019). On March 8, during the commemoration of Women's Day, a group of the relatives of victims of femicide and feminist collectives installed an *Antimonumenta (Anti-monument)*: a pink sculpture in the shape of a woman's symbol (♀), with a fist in the center as a sign of "resistance," and on its front face, two phrases: "We demand a national gender alert"[5] and "Not one more" (Sagastegui, 2019).

From the beginning of 2019 until April of that year, 424,867 complaints of alleged cases of sexual violence and harassment were filed using the hashtag *#MeToo* (Gómez, 2019b). In response, that same month, the capital government created a specialized group of the Procuraduría General de Justicia (PGJ) to investigate cases of femicide (El Universal, 2019b). In June, the Civic Culture Law was modified to sanction people who used obscene language against women. Despite these actions, the dissemination of cases of violence and the disappearance of female users of conventional cabs and *Didi* and *Uber* platforms increased in the media and social networks. Between July and August, three alleged sexual assaults committed by capital police officers, against a homeless woman, a woman in the Museum of Photography Archive, and a 17-year-old girl in the Azcapotzalco mayor's office, were publicized (Redacción AN, 2019).

The last case led nearly 500 women and members of feminist collectives to protest on August 12 in front of the Secretariat of Citizen Security (SSC). They demanded punishment for the police officers responsible for the rape. In the protest, they threw pink glitter against the secretary of the SSC, painted graffiti and phrases such as "We are bad, we can be worse," "rapist pigs," "They attack one and attack

---

[2] Galván (2019).

[3] Excélsior (2018).

[4] Data Cívica & Torreblanca (2019).

[5] According to the General Law on Women's Access to a Life Free of Violence, the gender alert consists of several emergency actions to confront and eradicate violence against women. In the CDMX, the alert was declared on November 21, 2019.

us all," and "They don't take care of us, they rape us." They also painted the uniforms of the police officers guarding the SSC facilities red. A group of women moved to the PGJ in Mexico City, where they painted phrases such as "officials' pigs," "corrupt police," and "We do not need to be brave, we need to be free" (Source, 2019). The PGJ authorities closed the glass doors of the building to prevent the entry of the activists. This aroused the anger of the women, so they broke down the doors and some of them smashed furniture in the reception area. Meanwhile, another group placed a pig's head at the entrance to the PGJ.

Both the attorney general and the mayor Mexico City described the events as "provocations" to which they were not going to respond. "We are not going to fall into any provocation […] They wanted the government to use violent methods just like the ones they used. And we for no reason are going to fall into provocations. Of course, there will be investigation files for what happened in the Attorney General's Office […] but the most important thing for us is not to fall into provocations", declared Mayor Sheinbaum in a press conference (Grupo Reforma, 2019).[6] On August 14, the event "Dialogue Zero Impunity and Absolute Justice for Women and Girls Victims of Violence" was held. The event was attended by authorities from Mexico City, the federal government, organizations, collectives, and feminist activists.

However, statements labeling feminists as "provocative" were rejected in social networks. Several feminist organizations and collectives issued a statement expressing their concern about the possible criminalization of protest being orchestrated by the government of Mexico City (Gómez, 2019c). Accordingly, they called for a set of marches in nine federal entities of the country under the slogans #NoMeCuidanMeViolan (#NMCMV) and #ExigirJusticiaNoEsProvocación (Aquino, 2019). On August 16, women in Mexico City gathered at various sites within the city, including the roundabout Insurgentes. Most were dressed in black, and some wore scarves or balaclavas with which they covered their faces. They carried banners with messages rejecting violence against women, some adorned with pink diamantine. During the rally, they shouted phrases such as: "I do believe you," "If they kill me, if they rape me, if they disappear me, destroy everything!" and "They are killing us, and you do nothing." In addition, different collectives read messages, danced, sang, and painted on walls and monuments.

Subsequently, the mobilization moved towards Reforma Avenue under the cry, "Down with the patriarchy that is going to fall, up with feminism that is going to win." During the tour, the interior of a Metrobus station was vandalized, furniture destroyed, and fires were lit inside and in front of it (La Silla Rota, 2019). Hours later, another group of protesters painted graffiti on a police station, entered it by force, and set it on fire. Several monuments in the city were painted with graffiti, including the emblematic Angel of Independence (El Financiero, 2019). The tourist place and meeting point for different expressions of joy and national discontent was

---

[6] On August 18, it was reported that no legal proceedings would be opened against the demonstrators. In the days prior to the march, a video was released showing that the young woman from Azcapotzalco had allegedly not been raped, revealing possible inconsistencies in her statements.

marked on its marble steps, metal sculptures, and stone columns, with phrases such as: "Not one less," "rapist police," "police-violence," "They'll never again have the comfort of our silence," "It's going to fall," "We're not to be trifled with," and "Mexico is a femicidal nation." Likewise, they used different symbols, such as ♀,Ⓐ or a symbiosis of both (Excélsior Tv, 2019). Aggressive acts also occurred in the subway, with beatings and graffiti on the clothes of men, journalists, animals and passersby who tried to participate, cover the events, or simply walking at that moment the demonstration was passing by.[7] Under the cry, "We were all of us," the demonstration died down as night fell.

Following the chronicles of that day the messages disseminated after the march were in favor of and against several topics. Messages such as: #NoMeCiudanMeViolan; #NiUnaMas; #feminicidios; #NoNosCiudanNosViolan, and #NosEstanMatando, rejected violence against women. Phrases repudiating the acts of violence against women in public spaces were used, with phrases such as #AsíNO; #AsíNoMujeres; #EllasNoMeRepresentan; and #AgredenAunoAgredenATodos. Other expressions were aimed at criticizing the performance of the head of the government, #CDMXinsegura #NoMásViolencia; and #RenunciaClaudiaSheinbaum. The march on August 16 was characterized by a type and magnitude of violence not seen before, above all, because the authority of the mayor was questioned and, to an extent, presidential authority was also being questioned. In this sense, the violent demonstrations not only put Sheinbaum in the public limelight but also catapulted presidential power itself to the forefront. The positions for and against violence by and against women, and the actions of public authorities, both local and federal, filled the news, the print and digital media, encapsulating public opinion. How did different audiences qualify the civil and anti-civil character of the August 16 march? What were the disputes generated in the Mexican civil sphere, in relation to the interpretation of the violence that took place in the march? How did the civil sphere expand or contract after these events?

5.2 Women's Illegitimate Violence

Public opinion, which judged the acts of "violence" during the mobilization led by the #NMCMV as civil or anti-civil, agreed that women live submerged in different forms of violence both in Mexico City and in the rest of the country. This sentiment was reflected in the newspapers *Milenio, Reforma, El Universal, Excélsior* and *La Jornada*. Furthermore, they highlighted different causes for this situation, such as gender inequality, the erosion of community relations, as well as the fracturing of the social fabric and the survival of the macho culture (Rodríguez, 2019a; Patrón,

---

[7] La Vanguardia (2019). https://www.youtube.com/watch?v=DsEcFCn1Nkg; Milenio Digital (2019). https://www.youtube.com/watch?v=ES2OcfGJXCo; Imagen Noticias (2019). https://www.youtube.com/watch?v=jrYDcCY_DrU.

2019; Guerra, 2019; Güemes, 2019; Niño de Rivera, 2019; Berman, 2019). The news columns were in agreement that the different forms of violence put women's physical and psychological integrity at risk and that they were a consequence of structural violence and heteropatriarchal values in Mexican society (Patrón, 2019; Semo, 2019; Ávila, 2019, Hope, 2019). In general, they recognized the multicausal character behind violence against women (Gómez, 2019a; Zamarripa, 2019; Rocha, 2019; Gil Antón, 2019). The state was accused of being a perpetrator of violence, particularly by failing to investigate and punish aggressions against women (Pérez, 2019; Zárate, 2019; Tello, 2019; El Universal, 2019a; González, 2019; Reneaum, 2019).

In the news columns, solutions were proposed, such as free self-defense classes for women (Fouilloux, 2019), the holding of a national conversation to think about how to confront the problem (Bonnafé & Calero, 2019), the promotion of cultural change, and a justice policy to end impunity and misogyny (Gómez, 2019a, Krauze, 2019b; Carbonell, 2019; Beltrán del Río, 2019). The goal, it was pointed out, should be to move from pain and anger to institutional changes (Ramírez, 2019). Although there were concurrences in the diagnoses and the solutions, there was little consensus in characterizing protest civil or anti-civil according to the motives, relationships and institutions of those who participated painting monuments or destroying furniture in the urban space.

For those who questioned the mobilization under the #NMCMV banner that ended in several acts of intervention, Mexico City was at times submerged in "vandalism" unleashed by the "psychosis" generated by the alleged rape of the young woman in Azcapotzalco. With this type of statement, it was suggested that behind the attacks on public services and certain monuments, there were deeply irrational motives, lacking a rational evaluation of the situation. From this evaluation, which characterized women as profoundly anti-civil, it was made clear that they were not autonomous women, but dependent on their emotions. Nevertheless, there were those who catalogued the violence that was unleashed during the #NMCMV as a rational, strategic and calculated response, who assumed that aggression toward the city was the only way to combat the violence they were experiencing. In this way, it was suggested that the violence experienced that day in the city was the result of having placed their interests above the rest of the city's inhabitants. Thus, social networks and media outlets such as the press and radio spread the idea that by destroying the city they could secure the attention of the authorities, regardless of whether they trampled on the rights of others. For some journalists, particularly from *Milenio, El Universal, Excélsior* and *La Jornada*, respectively at the center, right, and left of the national political spectrum, in the future, "feminist vandalism" should be added to the landscape of violence in the country's capital (Cueva, 2019).

It was assessed that the graffiti and vandalism were incomprehensible and contradicted the essential request to end violence against women (Quiroz, 2019; Cárdenas, 2019). The women who participated in the vandalism of public real estate were described as people who operated in the same logic of the relationships that criminals establish among themselves: aimed at "spreading vandalism." It was argued that it was a contradiction for the feminist movement to demand an end to impunity for rapists, murderers and stalkers, when they demanded impunity for the acts they carried out. In this interpretation, the women sustained relationships considered uncivil: based on complicity, suspicion, selfishness and deceit. While it is true also from this interpretation that the acts of "vandalism" perpetrated under the banner of the #NMCMV could not be compared to the murder of a woman, both sought to escape punishment for their illegal acts. Smashing furniture and public offices—just like femicide—originated from contempt for the rule of law. Thus, it was stated that both the femicide and the one who destroys the city act under the certainty that they will not and should not be punished (Beltrán del Río, 2019), and both deserve impunity.

From this interpretation, it was not convenient to minimize the vandalism of women during the #NMCMV, because it was not so serious, and it could not be compared to rape or femicide. With this statement, they were trying to point out that institutions should move in a biased and differentiated way, that they should operate in an arbitrary and exclusionary way for the benefit of one person or group. In other words, feminists, in defending women's violence during the #NMCMV, do nothing more than call for the impunity granted to rapists and perpetrators of femicide. Some editorial spaces warned that the argument, "The graffiti are erased, the dead are not," results from a 'false dilemma" that presents two options as mutually exclusive. If the graffiti prevented murder or violence against a single woman, there would be utilitarian reasons to defend the vandalism, but that was not the case. Some also argued that the violence of the protest was gratuitous and tainted a just demand, especially from the pages of the liberal newspaper *Reforma* (Bartolomé, 2019; Sarmiento, 2019). It was demanded, particularly from the columns of the centrist newspaper *El Universal*, that the authorities investigate and punish those responsible for the riots (Zavala, 2019). It was not possible that a police station was set on fire or public transport stations damaged without a subsequent judicial process (Döring, 2019; El Universal, 2019a). If something was not done against vandalism, it would be clear that the government had lost control of the city (Zavala, 2019). From this reading, women's violence was oriented toward establishing a relationship with institutions marked by pressure to obtain a particular benefit, fair certainly, but outside the legal framework.

For the critics of the actions taken during the #NMCMV—all of them speaking in *El Universal*—the destruction of the monuments did not represent "true feminism." Vandalism does not have and has not had a role in changing any society, they opined. Violence as an irrational act, served in this sense to contaminate the movement, especially because it always tends to polarize the citizenry (Gutiérrez, 2019). However, there were other positions that suggested that some of the young women who participated in the acts of destruction were part of political groups with diverse interests. In other words, they were infiltrators who aimed at discrediting the protest (Cedeño, 2019). The presence of a PRD shock group was alleged (Gómez, 2019b), and collectives of anarchist feminists, young people who had appeared on the urban scene during the inauguration of Enrique Peña Nieto in 2012 (Serrano, 2019). With these points, an attempt was made to contaminate the #NMCMV by warning that it was a mobilization partly manipulated by interests alien to feminism and women's causes. Thus, the women who participated in the "vandalistic" acts were categorized as subject to hidden social powers and, therefore, bearers of anti-civil elements: they watch over particularistic and selfish interests, which move from suspicious relationships and seek to mobilize institutions for the benefit of a particular group of society.

On the opposite side, it was also affirmed, from *El Universal* itself and from the leftist *La Jornada*, that the riots had been provoked by women tired of the violence to which they were subjected. It was estimated that their anger and weariness emanated from violence that stained a noble protest and operated in detriment of the social support they sought (Serrano, 2019). Therefore, it was considered necessary not to idealize violence, since it only brings more destruction, aggression, and social losses. From this position, it was argued that violence proffers a negative identity to the movement and could thus affect its cohesion. Some recommended curbing violence before it became an efficient means, institutionalizing itself as a normalized mechanism of collective vindication (Woldenberg, 2019). It was necessary to remember that "women's war is peace"; if they could manage to control and tame violence, "never turning the other cheek," they would be able to access the love and justice they sought (Bellinghausen, 2019). From this reading, it was judged that women who exercise any type of violence were actually contaminated by the elements of anti-civil behavior, characterized by irrationality, and, therefore, subject to their emotions. They were women who establish relationships marked by opacity, selfishness, and deference, seeking that laws and institutions protect them, but demanding for them a differential and tailored treatment for their exclusive benefit. In other words, from these voices within public opinion, the women were participating in acts of "violence" under the banner of the #NMCMV, a movement with legitimate demands, but ones set in motion by anti-democratic actions.

5.3 Women's Legitimate Violence

For another part of public opinion, particularly in the downtown newspapers, *Milenio*, *El Universal*, and the liberal daily *Reforma*, the expressions of anger and rage, as well as the alleged vandalism against monuments and furniture in the urban space, only exposed the conditions of structural violence, male domination, racism, and classism faced by women. The anger of the young women unveiled the conditions of violence under which they live and, above all, the indifference of the government in addressing their demands (Guerra, 2019). To stigmatize the protest was to evade the state of precariousness to which women in the CDMX have been subjected (Zamarrón, 2019; Zamarripa, 2019; Domínguez, 2019). From this interpretation, the violence that women exercised against buildings and monuments was motivated by a "natural" response of indignation, that is, driven by the feeling that the exclusion they suffer is undeserved or because they assume that there is a degradation of their condition as persons and citizens. Violence under these conditions was justified to the extent that it was the most appropriate response to express their weariness in the face of the different forms of violence they experience every day in social spaces.

In this tenor, some editorials, specifically from *Reforma*, *Excélsior*, and *La Jornada*, that is, from the right to the left passing through a liberal perspective, asked themselves: "Why do the graffiti affect us more than the thousands of women killed for reasons of hate in the present decade? Isn't this a manifestation, precisely, of an androcentric culture?" (Patrón, 2019). With this statement, those who judged the forms of expression of the #NMCMV as legitimate attributed to those who were outraged by the "violent" behavior of women anti-civil components linked to heteropatriarchy. Clearly, they valued the protection of monuments and buildings more than the lives of women. Similarly, it was argued that walls can be repainted, but women who die cannot come back to life (Islas, 2019). In this sense, it was suggested to leave the graffitied monuments as proof of the unmet demand to end violence against women (Catón, 2019; Azar, 2019). It was stated that by painting the Angel of Independence, a monument was rewritten in order to "invert –and appropriate–its symbolic efficacy [...]: it is the signature of those who at the foot of that Angel, refuse to become its ruins" (Semo, 2019). According to this interpretation, the demands for civil reparations had to be left exposed in the city as a testimony to the necessity for the institutions of both federal government and of Mexico City to act immediately to stop violence against women and femicide. In short, the city sought to guarantee the permanence of a series of slogans and intervened monuments as a reminder of the need to include and expand the logics of solidarity toward women.

The violence in the protest was justified as a valid expression of being "fed-up" (Ávila, 2019; García, 2019; Rocha, 2019). It was argued, by *El Universal* and *Excélsior*, that those who believed that the movement is legitimate in its substance, but not in its violent expressions, were wrong (Pérez, 2019). The movement was qualified as the expression of the "fury" of women who have decided to give a "slap in the face" to a government that has no "gender conscience," and is incapable of protecting women. The march could thus be understood as an act of rebellion against the inability of the Fourth Transformation to change the country, and the desire to sustain a misogynist vision of society (Pascoe, 2019). In this way, it was directly linked to presidential power, and not only to the government of Mexico City. Likewise, it was pointed out that the city government, despite its leftist and progressive tendencies, sustained an institutionality based on exclusion and arbitrariness, leaving unprotected a sector of the population that is being violated and murdered.

This logic underpinned some voices within public opinion, especially from the center of the political spectrum in *Milenio* and *El Universal,* as well as the liberal newspaper *Reforma*, warned that the violence and the outrage that unfolded across the city were proportional to the size of the indifference of the authorities (Aguilar, 2019; Berrueto, 2019; Zamarripa, 2019; Loaeza, 2019; Editorial El Universal, 2019b). What could be expected—warned one commentator—when violence brings out anger: "That woman in Mexico City would go out to protest quietly because that way they would look prettier? That instead of beating up shop windows they would hand out flowers to men?" (Becerra-Acosta, 2019). Similarly, other journalists judged that it was not with good manners that attention would be given to the problem. From this interpretation, the vandalism displayed by feminists was minimal compared to what they faced at work, at school, at home, and on the street (Guerra, 2019; Güemes, 2019). These protests showed that in the country there had been a generational change in feminism, in which "fear and "bravery," public denunciation, and hidden faces now speak (Zamarripa, 2019).

In this set of interpretations within public opinion, the imputations on the alleged civil and anti-civil behavior of the women who mobilized under the slogan #NMCMV gave rise to a new semantics that linked violence with attributions of civil virtues and non-violence with civil vices. Thus, anger, slogans, destruction of public space, misbehavior, vandalism, and the courage to take to the streets represented civil characteristics, while calm, silence, gifts, good manners, civility, and cowardice were considered characteristic of anti-civil behavior. In this way, feminism could only advance by showing courage and marking the city by altering its monuments and attacking its public buildings.

This perspective explains why some voices tried to imprint a revolutionary value on the march, since it was considered an attempt against the system of exclusion and intimidation that reigns over women. Moreover, according to some journalists, the protest unleashed the annoyance of the defenders of heteropatriarchal domination, depicting those who painted monuments or vandalized furniture "vandals" and "criminals." Accordingly, as reflected in *Reforma*, men in power should understand that a revolution seeking to transform the vulnerability of women cannot "follow the rules of etiquette dictated just by those who are responsible for the horror" (Volpi, 2019). In fact, those who label the women who protested "feminazis," do so to contaminate what they consider a threat against their interests. "Feminazi" is the postmodern version of the danger posed by the Amazon figure: "violent, armed women who live or want to live in closed societies that exclude men." "Amazons" and "feminazis," however, are myths in the minds of those who fear losing control over women (Turrent, 2019).

The above-described positioning sought to account for the civil nature of disruption, confrontation, and the value of subverting public order. It was clear in showing how the protagonists of the #NMCMV were not afraid to offend, or to damage public and private property. These acts were assumed as radical because, although they broke the law, they were not considered illegal actions. In this sense, violence was legitimated in terms of civil discourse. What was interesting about this positioning was that anti-civil behavior was attributed to the head of the government. Sheinbaum was accused of neglecting the accusation that city police officers had sexually assaulted a minor. It was thus demanded that she make the functions of her office operate as a space of universalist understanding, of the organization of authority as the mayor of Mexico City.

In addition, it was pointed out that Sheinbaum had been unwise to accuse the first demonstrations of being provocative. Sheinbaum's intention to qualify the demand to guarantee prompt and expeditious justice to the alleged victim as illegitimate and impure was judged negatively (Gantús, 2019; Krauze, 2019a; Gómez, 2019b; Backhoff, 2019). According to some voices within public opinion, social anger increased when the police officers accused of rape were reinstated to their jobs, ostensibly not to violate their labor rights, and, further, when the city authorities hinted that perhaps the rape had not occurred. Both actions only confirmed, according to this position critical of the government, the inefficiency and institutional tactlessness shown by Sheinbaum (Kraus, 2019; Reneaum, 2019). Thus, the mayor was accused by journalists from *Reforma*, *El Universal*, and *Excélsior* of moving the city's institutions in an arbitrary, exclusionary and oriented way, to benefit a particular group, to the detriment of women who demanded civil redress.

Nevertheless, there were voices in *Milenio*, *Reforma*, and *El Universal* that considered Sheinbaum's decision to retract the accusations she made to the women protesters of aiming to provoke the institutions as honest and open. Similarly, it was applauded that she withdrew the investigations that had been initiated against the protesters with the aim of clearing responsibilities for the acts of "violence" in the city (Zamarrón, 2019; Puig, 2019; Gil, 2019; Gómez, 2019b). Thus, according to this reading, Sheinbaum desisted from pointing out what kind of mobilizations against gender violence were legitimate or not; she had flipped her position in less than 48 hours. By giving citizen (civil) status to the women's mobilization, a journalist for *La Jornada* pointed out, the mayor had demonstrated that she belonged to a left that does not criminalize protests and that understands why the latter has had a violent drift. By correcting her position, Sheinbaum had brought to the present her own history as an activist in the feminist struggle (Hernández, 2019).

For some commentators, both from the centrist newspaper *El Universal* and the leftist daily *La Jornada*, this turn away from confronting the protests was a sign that Sheinbaum was working in favor of guaranteeing better living conditions for women in Mexico City (Ackerman, 2019). Her position of not repressing the protests at all was seen as positive. As some journalists pointed out, that there were rumors that a "hunt for perpetrators of femicide and rapists" would soon begin in the city, since the mayor had decided to make this issue a central priority of her administration (De Manuelón, 2019), along with the administration's efforts to rebuild the city's social fabric (Rodríguez, 2019b). From this interpretation, the radical acts deployed by women under the banner of #NMCMV functioned as a wedge for Sheinbaum to shift her positioning from anti-civil to a perspective in which she acquired the characteristics of civil purity expected from a leftist ruler of a progressive place.

There were also voices within public opinion that insisted—especially from *La Jornada*, that despite Sheinbaum's change in discourse, one should not fail to distinguish between allies and adversaries of the feminist cause in the city and in the government of López Obrador. They suggested that some politicians sought through a "false feminism" to use the protests to "unfairly attack the most feminist government we have today in the Republic" represented by the figure of President López Obrador (Ackerman, 2019). With this statement, it appeared that an attack on Sheinbaum was an attack on the presidential power delegated to her. It was warned that the use of glitter—as a symbol of protest against police abuse—had fallen into the hands of the right to give a "soft blow" to the Fourth Transformation, both at the local and the federal levels, under the argument that right and left are the same (Ackerman, 2019). From this reading, the demonstrations that took place in the city were actually being manipulated by interests outside feminism, in order to affect not only the city's mayor, but also the president.

In the face of these voices, there were others that tried to underline that Sheinbaum's change of attitude was inauthentic and not very credible, so she was trapped in an anti-civil logic, perhaps very close to a position that the president himself sustained. From *Milenio, Reforma, El Universal* and *Excélsior*, it was insisted that the mayor had not been able to establish communication with women in the city, nor had she developed policies to guarantee women's right to a life free from violence, a position that had already affected the president's own legitimacy (Rueda, 2019; Zamarrón, 2019; Dresser, 2019; Editorial El Universal, 2019a; Loret de Mola, 2019). It was considered that Sheinbaum treated the alleged rape as an administrative problem, when in fact it was a government issue that implied showing that patriarchal structures are being dismantled by a group of young feminists (Ramírez, 2019). From this reading, the capital's administration was better prepared to repair the painted monuments and destroyed furniture, arresting those responsible for the aggressions to journalists covering the protest, than to solve the cases of violence against women (Islas, 2019; Dresser, 2019).

This interpretation of Sheinbaum's position was emphasized when she held a meeting with feminists to try to take forceful steps to address violence against women and femicide. The event with the feminists ended up showing Sheinbaum's insensitivity to govern and portrayed her as having in her mind an old vision of feminism. It was stated in *El Universal* that Sheinbaum summoned to said meeting only the feminists of the "old guard" and left out the younger ones—the most combative and the most annoyed by the inaction of the government (Loret de Mola, 2019). Sheinbaum did not realize, argued her critics, that it was the young feminists who are transforming the public life of the country and not the feminists of the past (Gómez, 2019b). In this way, one of the attributions found in the debate between *#MeToo* and *Autre Parole* was reproduced: between an "old" feminism, considered from this perspective as outdated in the face of the new demands of women, and a "new" feminism, which understands how to build spaces of freedom and women's rights in a very different way. A journalist from *La Jornada* estimated that the government of both Mexico City, headed by Sheinbaum, and the federal government, headed by López Obrador, should consider that there were two irreconcilable feminist movements: one that bets on modifying the functioning of the state to reduce violence against women and another that sees in the state the origin of violence (Semo, 2019). According to this perspective, the first movement is embedded in the current local and federal governments, and the second one takes to the streets to protest.

5.4   The Thin Border Between Civil and Anti-Civil

As can be seen in Table 5.1, the attributions of anti-civil contamination coming from public opinion against the #NMCMV were underpinned—as already highlighted above—by class and/or status referents, under the pretension of revenge and not justice, all the while alleging that these feminists were conservative women. Consistent with the system of civil impurity attributed by the president, if the plaintiffs were not linked to the #NMCMV, they were portrayed as inauthentic feminists. To these elements, two others were added. Feminists were considered inauthentic if they were seen as irrational, driven by emotions that trigger acts of violence. In this sense, feminists would only be considered authentic to the extent that they were seen as representing collective interests, demanding justice under established legal frameworks, seen as progressive actors who presented their demands in a rational and reasoned manner, without deploying any kind of violence and, above all, supporting the president and his power.

In contrast, Table 5.2 shows that the civil attributions made by the public to #NMCMV were underpinned by the same referents of meaning: sanctions, the political orientation of the women who participated in the mobilization, their position with respect to presidential power, the type of demands, and their opinion on the use of violence. As can be seen in the table, vandalism, the progressive character attributed to women, as well as their distance from presidential power were considered as civil attributes that typified feminists as authentic. Moreover, the fact that demands were made from a place of irrationality and emotion was seen as a positive irruption in the social order. However, it is worth noting that one factor in distinguishing between authentic feminists included age, rather than class or status position. Public opinion in this case highlighted that the younger people who participated in the protests, the more they behaved rebelliously and showed greater autonomy

Table 5.1 Anti-civil classification system attributed to *#NMCMV*

	Class/Status	Sanction	Women	Relationship with presidential power	Requests	Violent
Authentic Feminism	Collective interests	Justice	Progressives	Yes	Rational/ reasoned	No
Inauthentic Feminism	Particular interests	Revenge	Conservatives	No	Irrational/ emotional	Yes

Source: Own elaboration

Table 5.2 Civil classification system attributed to *#NMCMV*

	Age	Sanction	Women	Relationship with presidential power	Requests	Violent
Authentic Feminism	Younger	Vandalism	Progressives	No	Irrational/ emotional	Yes
Inauthentic Feminism	Older	Civility	Conservatives	Yes	Rational/ reasoned	No

Source: Own elaboration

from presidential power. In other words, vandalism and violence represented a symbolic resource to make themselves heard.

Based on these classification systems, it can be affirmed that the march had three effects. In the first place, it constituted a space of solidarity and agreement within public opinion on the need to address violence against women and femicide, to recognize that it is clearly a serious problem affecting the country. But at the same time, the issue was divided, as already shown in this chapter, between those who endorse and legitimize acts of violence in the demonstrations and those who consider that violence should be censured and women who have participated in these acts should be punished. Finally, there is an effort to link violent protest with presidential power and the mayor of Mexico City, seen as a figure directly linked to the violence.

The three effects were sustained in the translation made by the women who participated in the #NMCMV mobilization of their demands in terms of the universal codes of civil discourse. Violence represented the means through which the demands for a life without violence were civilly translated. The authorities were, in this sense, evaluated as reproducers of a violent order which, in order to make the authorities seem more inclusive, needed to be itself violated. Violence was perceived by some voices within public opinion, as a way of hastening actions in terms of civil reparation. They worked to ensure that Sheinbaum activated the functions of her office as a space of universalist understanding of the organization of authority as head of the government of Mexico City.

In this way, the violent actions of the protesting women became a wedge to open up institutional spaces considered closed to demands for fighting against violence and femicide. Accordingly, violence was experienced as a form of communication within the civil sphere about experiences and fears generated by a social context that was not very favorable to women's development. Therefore, they brought to public opinion a discussion in which the need to improve living conditions by extending the solidarity structures of the civil sphere was formulated. Those who qualified the march as a civil action, appealed in this way to achieve civil reparations. Destroying and painting the public space were interpreted as new forms of feminist justice seeking to rewrite the processes of social inclusion and solidarity.

But there were also some among the public that considered the violence exercised by the #NMCMV mobilization as not emblematic of the civil values that the "feminine" supposedly embodies. It was argued that women's gender status compels them to use peaceful and non-violent means. They tried to contaminate the protesting women by labeling them as irrational, dangerous, hysterical, and contradictory. They assessed them as incapable of exercising citizenship and autonomy by being at the service of their passions or, worse, at the service of political groups. They considered the protest a blow against Morena and, consequently, against presidential power. They were accused of feeding the idea that violence was the most effective means to demand justice and inclusion, and to ensure adequate mechanisms to guarantee any civil redress over and above the rule of law. Thus, the march was qualified by some as an expression of an inauthentic feminism that did not favor the implementation of universal values of civil order and therefore did not achieve inclusion and solidarity.

The local government, as well as some people with social power alleged that the #NMCMV mobilization was clearly manipulated by actors who had other interests. Sheinbaum's criminalization of the women's protests—despite the fact that she later retracted it—was interpreted as an act of authoritarianism aimed at disarming the legitimacy of the feminist protests. This discursive mood would be repeated in subsequent feminist mobilizations when presidential power was directly questioned as regards violence against women and femicide. The relationship between presidential power, refracted by the mayor of Mexico City, public opinion, and feminist movements in this first mass mobilization, in the context of a government that assumes itself leftist, showed how the attributions of civil virtues and vices would later be deployed in the face of women's demands to stop violence and femicide.

The #NMCMV succeeded in assigning anti-civil principles to the heteropatriarchal system and male sexual aggressiveness, translating demands for gender equality and respect for bodily integrity into civil redress that would eliminate domination, discrimination, and violence. The mobilization of the #NMCMV allowed for new protagonists and antagonists in the realm of public opinion, in a narrative of liberation that combats male oppression and expands spaces of solidarity and justice. This move generated a shift in which women went from being considered victims, to become heroes who recount their stories of resistance and struggle. Thus, the #NMCMV translated violence and femicide as anti-civil elements that can only be reversed through the recognition of women within the normative referents of civil inclusion.

Within public opinion, the recognition of violence and femicide was a reality, but not it was not necessarily so for the legitimacy of the bearers of the demands. There were those who accused the #NMCMV of bearing anti-civil attributes, because it was aligned neither with mayor of Mexico City nor with presidential power. A part of public opinion pointed out that the authorities had criminalized the protest and had failed to achieve civil redress. Another part believed the authorities had acted adequately, even appealing to the pure or civil character of the mayor and the president. The discourses competing to take over the meaning of the #NMCMV protest managed to place the problem of violence against women and femicide in the national arena. The debate managed to generate a discussion that questioned the very characteristics of feminist protest, but, above all, questioned the supposedly "natural" qualities of women as civil actors who demand the right to a life without violence. With this type of protest, public opinion in Mexico was experiencing the construction of new ways of defining the space of inclusion, solidarity, and civil membership.

5.5 Heroes and Anti-Heroes

In this chapter, we have shown how the violent actions deployed in the feminist march were effective in amplifying the voices of women and demanding that public opinion, as a symbolic representation that crystallizes the "public," show solidarity with their demands. The social mobilization precipitated a discussion on the need to change the institutions that are meant to care for and support the victims of violence and the relatives of women who have been murdered. In this way, the mobilizations have made it possible to echo the demands for civil reparations demanded by women. However, at the same time, there were disputes about the civil and anti-civil nature of the mobilizations, as well as about the real capacity of regulatory institutions to meet women's demands. The main achievement of the mobilization and the competition for attributing meaning to it lies in the fact that it brought the issue of violence against women to the center of public debate. It did so especially in news media and on social networks, sites through which cases of harassment and violence against women were exposed and discussed. Faced with the facts of femicide both in Mexico City and in the rest of the country, there was a concentrated response, with protests and claims in the street, along with discussions in the media about possible causes and solutions. One may speculate that these debates are not helping to reduce the cases of violence and femicide, but it is also possible to affirm that they have contributed to building and concretizing a new set of semantic innovations, in which women appear not only as victims, but also as heroes and anti-heroes. In the first case, they are judged as heroes because they tell their stories of harassment and violence while altering the civil order to guarantee themselves a space in it. In the second case, they are qualified as anti-heroes because they construct a story of their own that breaks established stereotypes and make use of questionable methods.

References

Ackerman, J. (2019, August 26). Feminist government. *La Jornada.* https://www.jornada.com.mx/2019/08/26/opinion/022a2pol

Aguilar, H. (2019, August 19). Women, the background of anger. *Milenio.* https://www.milenio.com/opinion/hector-aguilar-camin/dia-con-dia/mujeres-el-trasfondo-de-la-ira

Aquino, E. (2019, August 14). Diamantina against violence: women call for protests Friday in several cities across the country. *Animal Político.* https://www.animalpolitico.com/2019/08/protesta-diamantina-contra-violencia-mujeres

Ávila, A. (2019, August 20). Reasons to be very angry. *Excélsior.* https://www.excelsior.com.mx/opinion/opinion-del-experto-nacional/razones-para-estar-muy-enojadas/1331387

Azar, E. (2019, August 29). Let women NOT be silent. *El Universal.* https://www.eluniversal.com.mx/opinion/edgar-elias-azar/que-no-callen-las-mujeres/

Backhoff, E. (2019, August 24). Education, gender violence and government. *El Universal.* https://www.eluniversal.com.mx/opinion/eduardo-backhoff-escudero/educacion-violencia-de-genero-y-gobierno

Bartolomé, F. (2019, August 18). Templo Mayor. *Reforma.* https://www.reforma.com/templo-mayor-f-bartolome-2019-08-19/op162716

Becerra-Acosta, J. (2019, August 19). Angry women… and unpunished males. *Milenio.* https://www.milenio.com/opinion/juan-pablo-becerra-acosta/doble-fondo/mujeres-furiosas-y-machos-impunes

Bellinghausen, H. (2019, August 26). Women: Their war is peace. *La Jornada.* https://www.jornada.com.mx/2019/08/26/opinion/a10a1cul

Beltrán del Río, P. (2019, August 19). What is Leona Vicario's fault?. *Excélsior.* https://www.excelsior.com.mx/opinion/pascal-beltran-del-rio/que-culpa-tiene-leona-vicario/1331197

Berman, S. (2019, August 25) Breaking more glass. *El Universal.* https://www.eluniversal.com.mx/opinion/sabina-berman/romper-mas-cristales

Berrueto, F. (2019, August 25). Being a woman. *Milenio.* https://www.milenio.com/opinion/federico-berrueto/juego-de-espejos/ser-mujer

Bonnafé, J. & Calero, N. (2019, August 23). "#LeavingNoOneBehind". *Reforma.* https://www.reforma.com/sindejaranadieatras-2019-08-23/op162973

Carbonell, M. (2019, August 27). The nightmare of impunity. *El Universal.* https://www.eluniversal.com.mx/opinion/miguel-carbonell/la-pesadilla-de-la-impunidad

Cárdenas, L. (2019, August 20). However, they violate them. *El Universal.* https://www.eluniversal.com.mx/opinion/luis-cardenas/y-sin-embargo-las-violan

Catón. (2019, August 23). Extreme measure. *Reforma.* https://www.reforma.com/medida-extrema-2019-08-23/op162974

Cedeño, A. (2019, April 2). #MeToo or how to stop the fire of Rome in the post-truth era. *El Universal.* https://www.eluniversal.com.mx/columna/alonso-cedeno/nacion/metoo-o-como-detener-el-incendio-de-roma-en-la-era-de-la-posverdad

Cueva, Á. (2019, August 18). #NoMeCuidanMeViolan and #EllasNoMeRepresentan. *Milenio.* https://www.milenio.com/opinion/alvaro-cueva/ojo-por-ojo/nomecuidanmeviolan-y-ellasnomerepresentan

Data Cívica & Torreblanca, C. (2019, February 26). Is there an epidemic of kidnappings of women in CDMX. *Animal Político.* https://animalpolitico.com/analisis/organizaciones/el-foco/hay-una-epidemia-de-secuestros-de-mujeres-en-la-cdmx

De Manuelón, H. (2019, August 26). Hunt for femicides. *El Universal.* https://www.eluniversal.com.mx/opinion/hector-de-mauleon/caceria-de-feminicidas

Domínguez, X. (2019, August 20). They don't rape them, they kill them, call a spade a spade. *El Universal.* https://www.eluniversal.com.mx/opinion/xavier-dominguez/no-las-violentan-las-matan-las-cosas-por-su-nombre

Döring, F. (2019, August 18). Bullets, diamantine and punch. *Excélsior.* https://www.excelsior.com.mx/opinion/federico-doring/balas-diamantina-y-punetazo/1331078

Dresser, D. (2019, August 19). Provocators. *Reforma..* https://www.reforma.com/provocadoras-2019-08-19/op162711

Editorial El Universal. (2019a, August 19). Women: the opportunity. *El Universal.* https://www.eluniversal.com.mx/opinion/editorial-el-universal/mujeres-la-oportunidad/

Editorial El Universal. (2019b, August 25). Sorority vs. insecurity. *El Universal.* https://www.eluniversal.com.mx/opinion/editorial-el-universal/sororidad-vs-inseguridad

El Financiero. (2019, August 16). Women march against sexual violence in various states of the country; demand greater security. *El Financiero.* https://www.elfinanciero.com.mx/nacional/mujeres-marchan-contra-la-violencia-sexual-en-la-cdmx-exigen-mayor-seguridad

El Universal. (2019a, August 19). Congresswoman offers to clean up graffiti. *El Universal.* https://www.eluniversal.com.mx/opinion/periodistas-el-universal/la-4t-se-fusila-vicente-fox

El Universal. (2019b, April 7). Mexico City Attorney General's Office establishes special group to address femicides. *El Universal.* https://www.eluniversal.com.mx/metropoli/cdmx/procuraduria-capitalina-instala-grupo-especial-para-atender-feminicidios

Excélsior. (2018, December 5). Claudia Sheinbaum is sworn in as head of government of the CDMX. *Excélsior.* https://www.excelsior.com.mx/comunidad/claudia-sheinbaum-toma-protesta-como-jefa-de-gobierno-de-cdmx/1282855

Excélsior Tv. (2019) *This is how the Angel of Independence was left after the women's protest. 17/02/2020.* [YouTube Video, 4:40]. https://www.youtube.com/watch?v=zkxbCrSQDvE

Fouilloux, S. (2019, August 25). Suggestion for Sheinbaum and AMLO. *La Jornada..* https://www.jornada.com.mx/2019/08/25/opinion/002a2cor

Galván, M. (2019, November 25). 14 gender violence facts that explain women's anger. *Politica Expansión.* https://politica.expansion.mx/mexico/2019/11/25/datos-sobre-violencia-contra-mujeres-mexico

Gantús, F. (2019, August 18). Authorities, between omission and delegitimization of protest. *El Universal.* https://www.eluniversal.com.mx/opinion/instituto-mora/autoridades-entre-la-omision-y-la-deslegitimacion-de-la-protesta

García, S. (2019, August 20). AMLO's "happy, happy" people. *El Universal.* https://www.eluniversal.com.mx/opinion/salvador-garcia-soto/el-pueblo-feliz-feliz-de-amlo

Gil Antón, M. (2019, August 24). Diamantina in the Mexican school. *El Universal.* https://www.eluniversal.com.mx/opinion/manuel-gil-anton/diamantina-en-la-escuela-mexicana

Gil, G. (2019, August 22). 'Provocatrices' and 'infiltrators'. *Millennium.* https://www.milenio.com/opinion/gil-games/uno-hasta-el-fondo/provocatrices-e-infiltrators

Gómez, H. (2019a, August 20). We were all. *El Universal.* https://www.eluniversal.com.mx/opinion/hernan-gomez-bruera/fuimos-todas

Gómez, L. (2019b, April 11). More than 424 thousand complaints arrived on the MetooMx platform. *La Jornada.* https://www.jornada.com.mx/ultimas/sociedad/2019/04/11/llegaron-mas-de-424-mil-denuncias-en-plataforma-metoomx-4395.html

Gómez, N. (2019c, August 14). Protest is not provocation; They denounce the criminalization of the march 'They don't take care of me, they rape me'. *SDP Noticias.* https://www.sdpnoticias.com/local/cdmx/protesta-mujeres-me-cuidan-marcha-cdmx-destrozos-diamantina.html

González, J. (2019, August 28). Violence against women, some reflections. *El Universal.* https://www.eluniversal.com.mx/opinion/jose-gonzalez-morfin/violencia-contra-las-mujeres-algunas-reflexiones

Grupo Reforma. (2019). *It was a provocation. - Sheinbaum. 12/08/2019.* [YouTube Video, 1:25:05 minutes] https://www.youtube.com/watch?v=ebuuJLdCOFU

Güemes, C. (2019, August 20). A Mexico without women (but with other data). *El Universal.* https://www.eluniversal.com.mx/opinion/cesar-guemes/un-mexico-sin-mujeres-pero-con-otros-datos

Guerra, G. (2019, August 21). Vandalism with a cause. *El Universal.* https://www.eluniversal.com.mx/opinion/gabriel-guerra/vandalismo-con-causa

Gutiérrez, S. (2019, August 22). Aggression does not represent me. *El Universal.* https://www.eluniversal.com.mx/opinion/sofia-gutierrez-larios/la-agresion-no-me-representa

Hernández, J. (2019, August 19). Astillero. *La Jornada..* https://www.jornada.com.mx/2019/08/19/opinion/008o1pol

Hope, A. (2019, August 19). Why women are angry. *El Universal..* https://www.eluniversal.com.mx/opinion/alejandro-hope/por-que-estan-enojadas-las-mujeres

Imagen Noticias. (2019). *Women vandalize Metrobús and police stations in Mexico City | News with Ciro Gómez Leyva 16/08/2019.* [YouTube Video, 5:03]. https://www.youtube.com/watch?v=jrYDcCY_DrU

Islas, F. (2019, August 31). Equity in justice. *Excelsior..* https://www.excelsior.com.mx/opinion/opinion-del-experto-nacional/equidad-en-la-justicia/1333585

Kraus, A. (2019, August 25). Femicide and orphanhood. *El Universal.* https://www.eluniversal.com.mx/opinion/arnoldo-kraus/feminicidio-y-orfandad/

Krauze, L. (2019a, August 19). Claudia Sheinbaum: hunting ghosts. *El Universal.* https://www.eluniversal.com.mx/opinion/leon-krauze/claudia-sheinbaum-cazando-fantasmas

Krauze, L. (2019b, August 26). Men: a problem. *El Universal.* https://www.eluniversal.com.mx/opinion/leon-krauze/los-hombres-un-problema

La Silla Rota. (2019, August 16). Women protest vs. gender violence in CDMX; groups vandalize Metrobus and police station. *La Silla Rota.* https://lasillarota.com/nacion/protestan-mujeres-vs-violencia-de-genero-en-cdmx-grupos-vandalizan-metrobus-y-estacion-de-policia-protesta-mujeres-violacion-delincuencia/309217

La Vanguardia. (2019). *Women's anger erupts in Mexico City 17/08/2019.* [YouTube Video, 1:05]. https://www.youtube.com/watch?v=DsEcFCn1Nkg

Loaeza, G. (2019, August 20). Brillanteada. *Reforma.* https://www.reforma.com/brillanteada-2019-08-20/op162785

Loret de Mola, C. (2019, August 19). At least they should know how to do this. *El Universal.* https://www.eluniversal.com.mx/opinion/carlos-loret-de-mola/al-menos-esto-si-lo-deberian-saber-hacer

Milenio Digital. (2019). *Millenio reporter attacked at women's demonstration 16/08/2019.* [YouTube Video, 4:05]. https://www.youtube.com/watch?v=ES2OcfGJXCo

Niño de Rivera, S. (2019, August 23). In Mexico we consume violence. *El Universal.* https://www.eluniversal.com.mx/opinion/saskia-nino-de-rivera-cover/en-mexico-consumimos-violencia

Pascoe, R. (2019, August 26). The Awakening. *Excelsior.* https://www.excelsior.com.mx/opinion/ricardo-pascoe-pierce/el-despertar/1332530

Patrón, M. (2019, August 22). What is it that outrages us. *La Jornada..* https://www.jornada.com.mx/2019/08/22/opinion/016a2pol

Pérez, C. (2019, August 20). Perpetuators and perpetrators. *El Universal..* https://www.eluniversal.com.mx/opinion/catalina-perez-correa/perpetuadores-y-perpetradores

Proceso. (2019, February 1). Call for march in the CDMX against kidnapping and femicide. *Proceso.* https://www.proceso.com.mx/570071/convocan-a-marcha-en-la-cdmx-contra-secuestros-y-feminicidios

Puig, C. (2019, August 19). All the other women *Milenio.* https://www.milenio.com/opinion/carlos-puig/duda-razonable/todas-las-otras-mujeres

Quiroz, F. (2019, August 19). Incomprehensible, the hostile complaint against violence. *La Jornada.* https://www.jornada.com.mx/2019/08/19/opinion/002a2cor

Ramírez, G. (2019, August 19). Historical subject. *Milenio..* https://www.milenio.com/opinion/gibran-ramirez-reyes/pensandolo-mejor/sujeta-historica

Redacción AN. (2019, August 9). At least 3 sexual assaults committed by Mexico City police, between July and August; 2 agents prosecuted. *Aristegui Noticias.* https://aristeguinoticias.com/0908/mexico/al-menos-3-agresiones-sexuales-cometidas-por-policias-de-la-cdmx-entre-julio-y-agosto-hay-2-agentes-procesados/

Reneaum, T. (2019, August 31). The women's ¡ya basta! that resounded across the country. *El Universal.* https://www.eluniversal.com.mx/opinion/tania-reneaum-panzsi/el-ya-basta-de-las-mujeres-que-resono-en-todo-el-pais

Rocha, R. (2019, August 20). Femicides: national gender alert. *El Universal.* https://www.eluniversal.com.mx/opinion/ricardo-rocha/feminicidios-alerta-nacional-de-genero

Rodríguez, G. (2019a, August 16). Zero impunity for girls and women. *La Jornada.* https://www.jornada.com.mx/2019/08/16/opinion/016a2pol

Rodríguez, R. (2019b, October 9). Stories of a lawless city. *El Universal..* https://www.eluniversal.com.mx/opinion/raul-rodriguez-cortes/historias-de-una-ciudad-sin-ley

Rueda, A. (2019, August 19). What if I had marched with them. *Excelsior.* https://www.excelsior.com.mx/opinion/adrian-rueda/y-si-hubiera-marchado-con-ellas/1331209

Sagastegui, D. (2019, March 8). 8 activities to commemorate #8M throughout March. *Chilango.* https://www.chilango.com/ocio/dia-de-la-mujer-2019/

Sarmiento, S. (2019, August 19). Violence and women. *Reforma.* https://www.reforma.com/violencia-y-mujeres-2019-08-19/op162718

Semo, I. (2019, August 24). Block of notes. *La Jornada.* https://www.jornada.com.mx/2019/08/24/opinion/015a2pol

Serrano, H. (2019, September 23). AMLO: dealing with other people's blunders. *El Universal.* https://www.eluniversal.com.mx/opinion/hector-serrano/amlo-lidiar-con-pifias-ajenas

Source, D. (2019, August 13). Women protest against police abuses; "it was a provocation": Sheinbaum. *El Universal.* https://www.eluniversal.com.mx/metropoli/mujeres-protestan-contra-abusos-de-policias-fue-una-provocacion-sheinbaum

Tello, I. (2019, August 23). Violence against women: normalized and silenced. *El Universal.* https://www.eluniversal.com.mx/opinion/irene-tello-arista/violencia-contra-las-mujeres-normalizada-y-silenciada

Turrent, I. (2019, September 1). Women. And men. *Reforma.* https://www.reforma.com/las-mujeres-y-los-hombres-2019-09-01/op163501

Volpi, J. (2019, August 24). Diamond Revolution. *Reforma.* https://www.reforma.com/revolucion-diamantina-2019-08-24/op163028

Woldenberg, J. (2019, August 20). Violence no. *El Universal.* https://www.eluniversal.com.mx/opinion/jose-woldenberg/violencia-no

Zamarripa, R. (2019, August 19). Without regard. *Reforma.* https://www.reforma.com/sin-miramientos-2019-08-19/op162712

Zamarrón, H. (2019, August 18). Our tragedy, our police. *Milenio.* https://www.milenio.com/opinion/hector-zamarron/afinidades-selectivas/nuestra-tragedia-nuestra-policia

Zárate, A. (2019, May 31). Guerrillas, neither angels nor demons. *El Universal.* https://www.eluniversal.com.mx/opinion/alfonso-zarate/guerrilleros-ni-angeles-ni-demonios

Zavala, M. (2019, August 19). Impunity and lawlessness. *El Universal.* https://www.eluniversal.com.mx/opinion/margarita-zavala/impunidad-y-anarquia/

Chapter 6
A Day Without Us

Abstract This chapter illustrates the power of the #UnDíaSinNosotras (A Day Without Us) movement, which was organized as a national women's strike that challenged presidential authority. The strike served as a platform for feminists to express their rejection of the increasing rates of femicides and violence against women. However, it was also perceived by some as an attempt to undermine the federal government's legitimacy and potentially create conditions for a coup d'état. Public opinion reflected this contentious issue, with people either supporting or opposing the call for a national strike and the president's efforts to diminish its impact.

Keywords National women's strike · Presidential power · Populist left · Social power · Civil power · Civil repair

6.1 Contaminating the National Strike

On March 9, 2020, a national women's strike was held in Mexico, under the hashtag #UnDíaSinNosotras, organized by the collective Witches of the Sea. Women were invited to stay at home, with their absence in the public space as a way of denouncing the inaction of federal authorities in cases of femicide and violence against women. It was intended to be a protest that contrasted with the march to commemorate March 8, International Women's Day, which had been traditionally held annually. The call for the strike generated wide discussion among the public. The aim of this chapter is to analyze how two competing discourses disputed the meaning of the national strike in order to symbolically control its legitimate or illegitimate, pure or impure, character, in relation to certain codes of solidarity and social inclusion. From a part within public opinion, the strike was considered a means for feminist

L. A. Cardona Acuña, N. Arteaga Botello, *Feminism, Power and Public Opinion in Mexico*, SpringerBriefs in Sociology,
https://doi.org/10.1007/978-3-032-14141-5_6

collectives and independent women—qualified as civil—to express their disgust in the face of the increase in femicides. Another part within public opinion, which replicated the discourse of presidential power—considered the national strike inauthentic, with accusations that there were conservative groups, characterized as anti-civil, behind the action, who intended to undermine the legitimacy of the federal government and even provoke the conditions for a coup d'état.

As described in Chap. 2, in the first year of López Obrador's government at the federal level and Sheinbaum's government in Mexico City, there were various instances of violence against women and acts of femicide. At the end of 2019, Abril Pérez was murdered in the streets of Mexico City by a group of hitmen, apparently paid by her ex-husband, who had recently been released from prison and had tried to kill her months before. Abril had reported to the authorities in Mexico City that there were threats to her life by her ex-husband. Her death generated public outrage, and the case was widely covered by the media. The indignation over the case grew when, on January 14, 2020, the Attorney General of the Republic, Alejandro Gertz Manero, presented a bill to eliminate the criminal definition of femicide, suggesting that it generated "confusion" in classifying the murders of women.

However, what sparked tremendous public outrage was the murder and skinning on February 9, 2020, of Ingrid Escamilla, at the hands of her then intimate partner. Her murder was amplified because some media outlets published photographs of Ingrid's flayed body, apparently leaked by Mexico City police. The public was immediately outraged. The day after Ingrid Escamilla's death and the leak of the photos, journalists asked the president about the crime in his daily morning conference with the media. The president evaded the answer by stating that he preferred to talk about the raffle of the presidential plane that the previous government had bequeathed him and how the plane served as one of the strongest proofs of the excesses of the presidents that preceded him. Since his campaign for the presidency in 2018, López Obrador had promised to sell the presidential plane to recover the money and invest it among those who had the least resources. However, all attempts to sell it failed, so López Obrador decided to raffle the plane among the population, whom he invited to buy lottery tickets.

Some voices linked to López Obrador interpreted the death of Ingrid Escamilla as a provocation to make him look bad. Critics of the president pointed out that his apparent disdain for the murder showed his insensitivity to violence against women. Public opinion gradually became polarized as other acts of violence against women and femicide took place. Two days after the murder of Ingrid Escamilla, on February 11, the kidnapping of Fatima, a six-year-old girl, who was found dead only 4 days after her abduction, was made public. Days later, on February 17, López Obrador stated that the cause of the instances of femicide emanated from the "neoliberal model" imposed on the country in the mid-1980s. He added at the end of his speech that it was necessary to be careful with the media outrage over the death of what he called "the girl," since behind it were hidden conservatives disguised as feminists who did not intend to put an end to violence or femicide, but rather to destabilize his government.[1]

The following day, on February 18, the feminist collective Witches of the Sea called for a national women's strike on March 9 under the slogans #UnDíaSinNosotras, #ParoNacional, and #El9NadieSeMueve." Immediately, the wife of President López Obrador –Beatriz Gutiérrez Müller, enthusiastically supported the initiative on Twitter. However, hours later, she retracted it on the same social network and proposed to support another initiative called #Undiamásconnosotras. This initiative called on women to take to the streets on March 9 with a white scarf to show that "society supported her husband's government," as well as the eradication of violence against women.[2] On February 21, the president warned again that it was necessary to "be very careful" with the feminist protests; he assured that they were being manipulated to turn the people against him. He pointed out that these movements were a prelude to coup attempts, accusing that "conservative groups in Chile and Mexico have used social movements to commit coups d'état."[3] The collective Witches of the Sea then retorted: "Where is [the right wing]? [...] Is [the president] not realizing that this is a legitimate citizen's demand?"[4]

However, while the president continued to insist on the supposed conservative character of the feminist call, the feminists achieved an increasingly significant presence in the media and social networks, giving voice to the organizers and supporting their arguments. On March 3, López Obrador announced that on March 9, he would start selling tickets to raffle the presidential plane. Feminists who supported the strike interpreted this action as an attempt to diminish the media relevance of the call for a strike. However, the president said a day later: "I did not even realize, nor did I have in mind that Monday was the 9th, the strike, what is being promoted."[5] The following day, the Secretary of Public Function (SFP), Irma Sandoval, tweeted: "To shake the country this March 9, instead of staying at home tempted to wash dishes and mend clothes, let's go out and occupy the public space just for us."[6] This statement aroused expressions of both support and criticism, to which Sandoval responded: "What hurts the right wing is that we women walk beside the president [...] That is what makes them furious and aggressive and pulls their mask of *fakeministas*.".[7]

In this way, the presidential power and the voices within public opinion that supported it, tried to contaminate the feminist mobilization for a national strike, as an expression its anti-civil components of the civil discourse: people moved by particularistic interests, who had a hidden agenda that sought to organize a conspiracy

---

[1] Nájar (2020, February 21).

[2] Redacción El Universal (2020, February 21).

[3] Jardínez (2020, February 21).

[4] Yañez (2020, February 26).

[5] Infobae (2020, March 4).

[6] Díaz (2020, February 23).

[7] Redacción animal Político (2022, February 22).

against a presidential power that embodied in itself the popular will. The feminists who called for the national strike and the members of the public that supported them tried in turn to sustain its civil character and declared that the president was the one moved by motives, relations, and institutions characterized by sustaining a set of social powers.

This tension led Olga Sánchez Cordero, Secretary of the Interior, to organize a meeting on March 5 with all the women in the president's cabinet to demonstrate the president's commitment to feminist causes, and to indirectly show that the functions of his office truly operated under the universalist understanding of the organization of authority. In that meeting, Sanchez Cordero affirmed that "women are the priority of the Fourth Transformation." However, at the same time, she acknowledged that the call for mobilization and the strike expressed women's weariness with the violence they had suffered. She therefore proposed that it was up to the discretion of each federal government agency to join the strike or not.[8] These statements were interpreted within public opinion as a way of recognizing the civil nature of the strike.

As in other feminist mobilizations, the president oriented his efforts to show their civil impurity. The sector of public opinion in tune with presidential power declared that the feminists behind the strike possessed attributes considered anti-civil. The discourse concerning their status as true feminists re-emerged. Therefore, their motives were not considered sincere, and, consequently, their demands came under suspicion because they were mobilized by those who were apparently conspiring against the president. In this way, it was judged, from a column in *Reforma* and more accentuated in *La Jornada*, that the strike was driven by conservatives who had disguised themselves as feminists, who had never defended the gender agenda, or women's rights (Lozano, 2020; Hernández, 2020c; Galván, 2020a).

From this position within public opinion, aligned with presidential power, especially present in *La Jornada*, it was also pointed out that it was strange and suspicious that banks and large corporations supported the national strike, when it was evident that they were the ones who most exploited and plundered women in their workspaces (Galván, 2020d). In this interpretation, the support of banks and large corporations somehow confirmed the hypothesis that right-wing groups were behind the call for the national strike, which aimed at undermining the "dense legitimacy" that President López Obrador possessed (Linares, 2020a). Thus, the call for the national women's strike was interpreted from this side as substantially inauthentic, because it was subject to manipulation by social actors alien to the struggle of feminism and very close to the interests of powerful groups.

John Ackerman (2020), one of the most prominent ideologues of President López Obrador's project in the first years of his term, at the time a regular columnist for the newspaper *La Jornada*, charged that the strike was a bad copy of similar efforts such as Iceland's *"Day Off"* (1975) or the United States' *"A Day Without Women"* (2017). In contrast to the strike called in Mexico, those women's mobilizations took the

---

[8] Corona (2020, Marc 5).

public space in a decisive way and at no time suggested that women stay at home to protest. For Ackerman (2020), it was a contradiction that women were asked to stay at home when in Mexico the home is the space where women suffer the most violence and the effects of the power of heteropatriarchy. Consequently, this commentator pointed out, to have a strike in which women stayed at home was to condemn them irremediably to violence. His conclusion suggested that, with their protest, the promoters of the national strike actually had a distorted idea of what was really happening to women in the country. In terms of civil discourse, Ackerman activated the anti-civil codes that portrayed the feminists calling the strike as ignorant of women's living conditions, lacking empathy, and clearly unaware about the causes underlying violence against women.

For Ackerman (2020), the lack of knowledge that those calling for the strike supposedly had concerning conditions in which millions of women in Mexico lived was not surprising, since they came from middle- and upper-class sectors that did not represent the population as a whole, but only a small group. That is why, according to Ackerman, their discourse fit in with that of the right wing: traditionalist, classist, and conservative. In addition, he affirmed that "semantically" the organizers of the strike were in tune with heteropatriarchal ideology, and their intention was to undermine the government of López Obrador and not to change the living conditions of female victims of violence. Therefore, Ackerman concluded in his text, whoever joins the strike will irremediably support those who seek to overthrow the government that has worked the hardest for women. Ackerman activated the codes that sought to contaminate a certain group of feminists by declaring them inauthentic, by virtue of their class condition or skin color, much in the same way that the French female actors behind *Autre Parole* were accused (see Chap. 2), which, in the end, reproduced the domination of women.

Thus, critics of the strike assured, particularly in *El Universal*, a newspaper of the center, and *La Jornada*, on the left, that the strike would end up being a resounding failure, that most women would not participate, because they had noticed the presence of "pro-life feminists" and conservative Catholics (Galván, 2020b; Hernández, 2020d; Homs, 2020). From this view, López Obrador was aware of the problems faced by women, like no other president in the history of the country, so he would not punish any of those who decided to miss work (Galván, 2020c; La Jornada, 2020b). It was even claimed from this position that the president changed the date of the presidential plane raffle in order not to polarize and to allow even the right-wing groups behind the strike to demonstrate (Hernández, 2020d).

6.2 Purifying the National Strike

Those members of the public that supported the call for the national strike launched by the collective Witches of the Sea argued, contrary to presidential power, that López Obrador was insensitive and incapable of recognizing an authentic feminist expression that showed the vitality of civil society. It was noticed from all directions, from the *Reforma* newspaper on the left, *El Universal* at the center, and *Excélsior*, apparently from the right, that the president had expressed positions once heard from the most conservative movements in the country, to shore up their leadership by means of social polarization. By blaming neoliberalism for the incidence of femicide, it was warned, the president showed himself cold and indifferent to a problem that required a more humane political vision (Garfias, 2020; Woldenberg, 2020b). From this position, it was stressed that the president's cynicism was evident when he pointed out that he preferred to talk about the airplane raffle rather than about violence against women (Loaeza, 2020; Crespo, 2020; Rubinstein, 2020; Camargo, 2020b). Thus, the president was accused of embodying the elements of anti-civil actors: lacking empathy for human suffering, with a distorted perspective on violence and femicide, concerned with guaranteeing the continuity of his personal interests and, ultimately, fostering antagonism in order to reproduce a hierarchical institutional structure based on political loyalties.

A number of voices within public opinion –not only from newspapers of the center such as *Milenio* and *El Universal,* but also from the right such as *Excélsior* and the left such as *La Jornada*– criticized the president's call to recover unity and family values as the only response to violence against women (Puig, 2020a; Melgar, 2020). It was charged that these responses showed the conservative disposition of the president, reluctant to support leftist positions regarding feminism (Hernández, 2020b; Raphael, 2020b; Carreño, 2020b; Bellinghausen, 2020). In this way, in terms of the civil discourse, presidential power was characterized as a guarantor of non-civil principles of inclusion and solidarity, particularly those expressed within the family. It was a solidarity based on the principles of emotional loyalty and love, but not on civil respect, nor on critical principles; in the family there are strongly authoritarian relationships, not only between parents and children, but also between couples that conform to such values. Consequently, declarations by the president suggested that it was necessary to reestablish the restricted patterns of solidarity found in family ties in order to avoid femicide and violence against women.

At the same time, it was pointed out, by newspapers located to the right and center such as *Excélsior, Milenio* and *El Universal*, that López Obrador contaminated the strike as a polarization strategy that would guarantee an increase in his presidential power. They pointed out that this allowed him to claim that a "soft coup" was being plotted against him (Garfias, 2020; Crespo, 2020) and thus justified the disqualification of the feminist mobilization for a national strike. Some political news columns charged that the president and his "corifeos" (leaders) saw behind the strike the black hand of the right and conservatives (Gamés, 2020), ready to initiate a "proto-fascist" hunt for the Witches of the Sea (Marín, 2020b). In this view, an attempt was made to contaminate the president by accusing him of being motivated by anti-democratic principles, with a perverse vision of the motives of what he considered his political opponents and showing the arbitrary, hierarchical, and exclusionary face of the presidential institution.

Within public opinion, as a normative referent of civil society discourse, rightwing, liberal and left-wing positions all considered that the president was wrong to assert that the feminist mobilization for a national strike was manipulated. In columns published by *Reforma, Excélsior, La Jornada, Milenio* and *El Universal*, it was argued that there was neither a black hand, nor a conservative party, nor a reaction behind the women's mobilization (Aristegui, 2020b; Loaeza, 2020; Romero, 2020a; Hernández, 2020b; Raphael, 2020b; Ordorica, 2020; Rodríguez, 2020a; García, 2020a; Dresser, 2020; Aguayo, 2020). Similarly, it was pointed out that it was ridiculous to consider that there was a destabilizing factor behind each victim of violence or family members who had suffered some loss due to a femicide act (Crespo, 2020). Femicide should not be considered entirely a media phenomenon encouraged by conservatives to destabilize the supposed government of the Fourth Transformation (Cueva, 2020a). From this reading, it was considered that the strike was a citizens' initiative, beyond the left or the right (Maza, 2020; Cueva, 2020a; Muñoz, 2020). Accordingly, the feminist mobilization was actually a clear expression of civil power seeking morally and legally just reparations in the face of a clear and growing scenario of violence against women.

In this interpretation of public opinion, in which columnists from *Reforma, Excélsior, La Jornada* and *El Universal* coincided, it was even suggested that the president seemed obsessed with discrediting any social and civil mobilization that did not emanate from his person or that was not directly linked to his power (Belaunzarán, 2020b); it seemed that he assumed himself as the only voice capable of morally guaranteeing the crystallization of the popular voice. This position set up a scenario in which no one could substitute in this role (Cossío, 2020). Even when feminists were not against him (Romero, 2020b) the president seemed to resent being questioned regarding what he says and considers prudent (Bellinghausen, 2020). If he did not assume the feminist protest as his own –it was warned—he would look like a chauvinist and a conservative (Jáuregui, 2020b). In this way, the president was trying to translate his social power into civil power, this translating the requirements for participation in civil society into restrictions and exclusion mechanisms.

A part of public opinion –represented by both liberal newspapers such as *Reforma* and left-wing newspapers such as *La* Jornada– called on López Obrador to recognize the diverse and dissident voices of his supporters: pro-abortion, anti-abortion, women of the left and the right, rich and poor, as well as the commander of the Zapatista Army of National Liberation (EZLN). In such diversity, one could testify to the women's act of freedom and their capacity for sorority (Peredo, 2020b; Orozco, 2020; Gómez, 2020b; Gordillo, 2020; Cárdenas, 2020). Faced with the presidential image, the columnists argued, women were social actors who expressed and condensed the values of civil power, insofar as they showed themselves, beyond the categories of class, race, hierarchical, or political position, as fully autonomous subjects, motivated by principles of justice, and above all, capable of building trustworthy, open, sincere, and deliberative bonds that demanded equitable and inclusive institutions regulated by law.

It was further interpreted that the president should be clear that the rapist or perpetrator of femicide does not ask the victim whether or not she is in favor of abortion, whether she is right or left (Belaunzarán, 2020b). Classifying women—warned Jáuregui (2020b)—as left (pro-government) and right (anti-government), could be interpreted as harassment: "I am not interested in your position, but in the position, I force you to take." It must be recognized, stated Lomnitz (2020), speaking in in *La Jornada*, that there are feminists of all kinds, as well as of different sexual preferences: that is indeed the liberating and revolutionary character of feminism. Irma Sandoval was also questioned for implying that it was not necessary to stay at home because that "generated the temptation to wash clothes and dishes." as if women automatically performed those activities at home. Columns in *Reforma* and *El Universal* accused the Sandoval of stigmatizing women who supported the strike as *fakeminists* (Sarmiento, 2020; González, 2020b).

In the center and liberal media, such as *Reforma* and *El Universal* (Aguayo, 2020; Crespo, 2020; Sefcovich, 2020), it was argued that there was even a tension within the government and the ruling party regarding how to categorize the women and the feminists promoting the national strike. From this interpretation, the press conference of the women's cabinet called by Secretary of the Interior Olga Sanchez Cordero showed that the call for the strike was an expression of the anger of women against the violence they were suffering and against femicide and not a moral and political sanction against the president. Through this cabinet meeting, the government tried to satisfy its sympathizers attracted by the strike and who could begin to doubt the president's empathy for women. This tension was even perceived by the president's own wife: at the beginning, she supported the strike and, shortly after, she reacted against it and presented another alternative to protest violence against women and femicide. This behavior crystallized the tension among the president's feminists to typify the strike as pure or impure. From this reading, the women in the president's cabinet tried to show that the president was sensitive to the civil power that seemed to be building around the feminist mobilization in favor of the national women's strike.

However, there were columnists from *Milenio*, *Excélsior* and *La Jornada*, the first two on the center and right of the political spectrum and the second on the left, who asserted that this tension within the government apparatus and López Obrador's political party was non-existent. López Obrador and his cabinet knew that women were angry about the lack of policies against femicide (Melgar, 2020), but they did not know how to face the social criticism that evidenced that. By assuring that the strike was not a criticism of the president, they were seeking to hide the failures of the current administration (Marín, 2020a; López Dóriga, 2020; Hernández, 2020e). Furthermore, it was serious that government officials assured that the women of the country supported the president, assuming themselves as representatives of all Mexican women, not possible in a plural and democratic society (Esquinca, 2020). Those from the "left" or "progressive" and "revolutionary" positions, believed they had the moral authority to define who can support or participate in the strike, were mistaken (Fernández de Cevallos, 2020). In this positioning of public opinion, the narratives of civil and anti-civil purity could not be subject to the monopoly of a political actor, in this case the president. It was judged in at least one column of *Reforma* that neither the president, nor his wife's attempts, nor those of the supposed feminists around him, would be able to stop the strike (Jáuregui, 2020a).

From the newspapers at the center, *Milenio* and *El Universal*, as well as at the left, like La *Jornada*, it was said that the national strike would end up showing the strength of women in all areas of social life (Revueltas, 2020; Baz, 2020; Blanco, 2020). The voices of public opinion empathetic to this reading from a left linked to the president, all of them from *La Jornada* and *El Universal*, warned that it did not matter if the strike was politicized (Anderson, 2020), if by doing so it was transformed into an act that would significantly and profoundly alter Mexican society (Muñoz, 2020; Concha, 2020; Gordillo, 2020; Anderson, 2020). Therefore, it was a gender revolution that in the future would be remembered and never forgotten (Zamarrón, 2020) since there would be blood and destruction, which was inevitable in any revolutionary movement (Cueva, 2020b). From these critical interpretations of the president, it was emphasized that companies or employers should be prevented from "pink washing" (Puig, 2020b; Sarmiento, 2020) and thus curb the opportunism of political parties (Ramírez, 2020) to maintain the purity of the women's movement in favor of the national strike.

The competing positions for the control of meaning within public opinion with respect to the strike and its conveners were somehow reflected in a survey published by Mitofsky, which showed that the country was divided with respect to the strike. Forty-eight percent considered that the strike should be supported, and 42 percent said they were against it (Rodríguez, 2020b). This polarization was interpreted as a positive fact by some columnists of *La Jornada* and *Excélsior,* on the left and the right, respectively (Gómez, 2020a; Fuentes, 2020), to the extent that the discussion allowed for the socialization of the women's cause. In this way, the survey made public opinion appear homologous to the binary codes of civil society: it appeared as a reflection of the categories of the pure and impure provided by the discourse of civil society and, simultaneously, an application of these binary categories. In other words, it expressed what the public was unwilling to know in relation to a situation that had already been communicatively constructed with reference to the binary coding of the civil sphere.

6.3   Competition for the Control of Meaning

Part of the public opinion crystallized in *Milenio*, *Reforma*, *Excélsior*, and *La Jornada* considered that the strike was a success: things were changing in the country in terms of gender relations, so the strike laid the foundations for what was considered a new civilizational paradigm (Albarrán, 2020; Peredo, 2020a; Belaunzarán, 2020a; Aristegui, 2020a; Linares, 2020b). Most of the opinions noted that the women's response to the strike was broad, with diversity in terms of different social classes, ages, professions, and sexual orientations (Raphael, 2020a). Some celebrated that the mobilization developed outside the discourse and resources of the Fourth Transformation, to such an extent that the government did not understand what had occurred (Aguilar, 2020; García, 2020a, 2020b). Fortunately, as Camargo (2020a) put it, the polarizing and stigmatizing discourse of the president did not diminish women's participation. In this sense, the strike was read as authentic because it was able to mobilize support from civil society.

In contrast, for some voices within public opinion, from *El Universal*, for example, the president's image was affected because he did not know how the logics of social expression work in democratic societies (Aziz, 2020). If the president was conceived as the recipient of the popular will, it was warned, in the future, we would see a president bothered by any social movement that expresses itself and that is outside the gravitational field of his political control (Woldenberg, 2020a). However, other voices, from *La Jornada*, *El Universal* and *Milenio*, warned that the strike was as successful as the march of the previous day: both mobilizations expressed women's rejection of violence. In this way, the civil attributions given to the movement ended up confirming in the broad spectrum of political positions within public opinion that the women's mobilization was actually an expression of civil power (La Jornada, 2020a; González, 2020a; Güemes, 2020; Nacif, 2020; Malvido, 2020).

Public support for the president, however, maintained a position in which they tried to generate a narrative of pure and impure women in terms of their position with respect to presidential power. In this way, they sustained their critique of the anti-civil motives and ties of the women who supported and mobilized for the strike. In contrast, they pointed out that the women who had attended the traditional March 8 march for International Women's Day were made up of "radical left" and "progressive feminist" groups that had brought López Obrador to power. For these sectors of public opinion, the women were truly autonomous because they were in favor of the president, who had actually supported feminism throughout his political career. While it is true that in the March 8 mobilization, there were some small radicalized groups that had criticized the government, in reality, they were a minority that faded in the face of the broad support of women linked to the project of the country's Fourth Transformation (Galván, 2020e; Martínez, 2020; Carreño, 2020a; Hernández, 2020f).

Therefore, in the interpretation of public opinion linked to the president, the national strike was a failure, because most women in Mexico realized that the strike was led by conservative and right-wing groups. In fact, it was stated that the women who participated in the strike were those who bore a privileged life condition, who were part of the middle and upper classes that could afford the freedom to stop their public activity. In this sense, the strike did not contribute much to the feminist cause, noted Hernández (2020a) and Gasman (2020), columnists for *La Jornada*. Nevertheless, the dispute about the autonomous character (or not) of the strike left the idea that there are two types of feminism, according to Senator Monreal (2020), MORENA's senator of the republic and columnist for *Milenio*: a destructive one that accuses the president of representing patriarchy and a constructive one that shows the strength of women in working with the government. According to this interpretation, the world of women was divided into two camps. On the one hand, there were those who questioned the president and had no intention of collaborating with the government and were therefore characterized as irrational, conspiratorial and factional—all anti-civil properties. On the other hand, there were women who worked with the government: rational and realistic, open, sincere and direct, who seek inclusion, equality and the construction of inclusive policies for women—essential components to be considered civil actors.

6.4   Inclusive and Exclusive Membership

Despite all the controversies generated by the president and within public opinion, the strike generated positive effects in the communicative and regulatory institutions of the civil sphere. For one, it generated a broad space for discussion on the causes of violence against women and femicide. Furthermore, it reconstructed in a particular time and space the narratives of purity and civil impurity that can be found in the international debate about those who are truly feminist, who defend women unconditionally and from a universalist perspective of inclusion, and those who speak from particularist positions, centered on a limited vision of the feminine, at the service of interests outside feminism. In other words, it generated a debate about the very meaning of feminism. Finally, from the side of presidential power and the public opinion that supported it, it was made clear that everything that mobilized outside the gravitational field of the president should be considered as civilly contaminated.

The March 8 mobilization and march was assumed by some members among public opinion as an expression of civil values and principles; in contrast, the national strike confronted two discourses. The first one imputed anti-civil values to the strike, arguing that it was promoted by conservatives to destabilize the government, considered from this position as an expression of civil and democratic values. From this position in favor of presidential power, women were described as heteronomous actors incapable of freely exercising their citizenship because they were deceived by more intelligent and strategic actors, linked to conservatism and political reaction. Women were accused of reproducing the mechanisms that kept them dominated and subordinated to the home, a space characterized by hierarchical and heteropatriarchal relations. The strike was described as the expression of an inauthentic feminism, impure in civil terms, incapable of promoting inclusion and the generation of broadened citizen membership.

Those who supported the strike –from this reading– considered that the women who had called for it had just motives, were authentic, autonomous, and that, despite the diversity of their voices, they shared an interest in denouncing violence against women. The diversity of women's voices was necessary, it was affirmed from this position, even if they were not feminist, progressive and left-wing, because the intention was that women would join, regardless of party and ideological affiliations. Broadening the inclusion of female and male voices would, according to such an interpretation, produce a strong message to generate mechanisms for civil redress, expanded solidarity, and inclusive membership. Regardless of the conflicting visions, the competing discourses managed to situate both the problem of violence against women and femicide in the national spotlight, along with disputes over "authentic" and "inauthentic" feminism. The debate succeeded in generating a discussion that questioned the characteristics of feminist protest, the role of the government and the regulatory institutions of the civil sphere.

6.5   From Feminist Effervescence to the Pandemic

The national strike had mobilized different feminisms with enough strength to demand equity in care, equal opportunities, and reproductive rights, so it was constantly signified by those who opposed or defended it. It was a strike, like any symbolic action, open to interpretation and therefore its meaning could not be controlled by the narratives of contamination and purification of presidential power and public opinion. This inability to capture cannot be attributed to the clumsiness or political or ideological intelligence of those who made an effort to attribute a single meaning to the national strike, but to the fact that the latter is a social text with multiple readings that can be altered over time.

The strength of the mobilization called by the Witches of the Sea to carry out a national women's strike challenged presidential power presented as unquestionable by its political and social opponents. Public opinion echoed a debate in which the mobilization was characterized by its civil power in the face of a government that tried to question the authenticity and strength of those who supported the strike. Public opinion translated this dispute and the feelings it aroused both for and against the call for the national strike and the attempts of the presidential power to contaminate it. Thus, different ways of putting the universal referents of solidarity, inclusion, and women's demands for civil reparation into play, in the face of violence and femicide, were exposed. Clearly, women's demands for recognition as authentic social actors were presented as more inclusive. On the contrary, presidential power reflected instead the pretensions of political power to mark and typify women as subjects that did not deserve to be considered as valid citizen voices.

As can be seen in Table 6.1, the system of anti-civil attribution to the national strike within public opinion—as a normative referent of civil society discourse—was patterned by a set of representations that combined some of the components of the debate between #Metoo and *Autre Parole*. To contaminate the feminists and women behind the strike, class or status criteria (upper-class women) and racial (white women) were assigned to them. To this was added the political stigma of conservativism and, following the same criteria used in #NMCMV, a destructive character, hardly proactive and prone to violence. It was thus charged that the suggestion women stay at home was in tune with a certain status, race, political position, or type of demand. However, what operated as a central switch in the

Table 6.1 Anti-civil classification system attributed to the National Strike

	Class/ Status	Race	Women	Requests	Complaint	Relationship with presidential power
Feminists Authentic	Popular classes	Non-white	Progressives	Constructive	Public	Yes
Feminists Inauthentic	Upper classes	White	Conservatives	Destructive	House	No

Source: Own elaboration

designation of the character of "inauthentic" feminists was whether they sustained a conflictual relationship with presidential power. "Authentic" feminism was assigned to women of popular classes, non-white, considered progressive, and, therefore, in a leftist government, their demands were circumscribed in constructive terms. Moreover, they were women who take to the streets and, of course, have a relationship of collaboration and support for presidential power.

In contrast, Table 6.2 shows how the system of civil attribution to the national strike within public opinion worked also in the opposite direction. The call for the strike involved and called for the participation of all social classes and status groups, with women of different races participating. Indeed, it was precisely the plurality of classes and skin color that lent a progressive character to the march and to the women who would and did participate in it. In this sense, it was considered that the broad underpinning through which the strike was sustained gave account of the reasonable and reasoned character of the call, because leaving the public space without women was a way of evidencing their strength and presence in social life. But, above all, it was the distant relationship with presidential power that allowed those who supported the national strike to construct its character as a mobilization of authentic women and feminists. In contrast, inauthentic feminism came from a group that asserted forcefully that only women of the popular classes, non-white, and supportive of presidential power, could claim to represent all women. At the end of the day, this attribution turned them, according to voices critical of presidential power, into conservative expressions, motivated by irrationality, emotionality, and loyalty to presidential power: hence the demand to take to the streets with a white handkerchief to show support for President López Obrador.

Beyond this dispute, the main achievement of the strike was that, in the competition for meaning, the issue of violence against women was placed at the center of public debate, particularly in the media and social networks, in which cases of harassment, stalking, and femicide were exposed and discussed. Beyond disqualifications, discussions were raised in the media about possible causes and solutions to the problems faced by women. Despite the fact that in the days following the national strike, Mexico was quarantined by the Covid-19 pandemic, it is possible to observe the articulation of a set of civil values nurtured by women with trajectories, lineages, and worldviews that do not respond to the traditional figures of feminism,

Table 6.2 Civil classification system attributed to the *National Strike*

	Class/Status	Race	Women	Requests	Complaint	Relationship with presidential power
Authentic feminists	Inter-class	Multi-racial	Progressives	Reasonable/reasoned	Leaving public space	No
Inauthentic feminists	Popular classes	Non-white	Conservatives	Irrational/emotional	Going out on the street	Yes

Source: Own elaboration

but who tell their stories of harassment and violence while seeking to ensure that their voices are heard. It is not that these discourses did not exist before, but the dispute around the national strike made them visible, generating a debate in which feminist horizons were broadened. The confinement to which the population had to submit to protect itself from the pandemic did not prevent women from continuing to denounce cases of domestic violence, harassment, and femicide.

The national women's strike of 2020 became a symbolic referent for women's struggle against violence and femicide. From then until the date this book was completed, a march takes place every anniversary on March 9. The date is considered a turning point in the feminist struggle that sought to distinguish itself from the traditional mobilization occurring on March 8, now considered an expression trapped in the governmental line. In this sense, March 9 assumed itself at first as a demonstration more linked to civil society and independent organizations. However, little by little, it has been institutionalized in order to make the two expressions of feminist protest coexist. In fact, the slogan promoted by some feminist organizations appeared, "On the 8th everyone takes to the streets, and on the 9th, nobody moves."[9] The Chamber of Deputies declared that every March 9 be considered a "National Day without us"[10] under the slogan "On the 9th, nobody moves."

However, despite this process of institutionalization, the women who demonstrate on March 8 regularly march to the zocalo (central square) in Mexico City. Since the events of 2020, the federal government has decided to wall off the national palace so that it will not be defaced with graffiti. Within public opinion, this action has been read as a fact that confirms the closed mindedness of the president in attending to the demands of various feminist groups. Faced with these accusations, López Obrador has pointed out that since the feminist protests strangely began during his term in office, they should be read as strategies to attack his person and his presidential investiture. In 2022, he stated: "[B]efore there were no such protests, they began in my government." Regarding the decision to wall up the national palace, López Obrador opined.

> They [conservatives] are upset because a fence was put up to prevent violence. We don't want anyone to get hurt; we have to take care of the women and those who participate in the demonstrations. Because imagine a Molotov bomb exploding on whoever uses it. We don't want that, we love life, we want peace.[11]

Thus, the president insisted that the expressions of civil power were nothing more than manifestations of social power that wanted to undermine his legitimacy, rooted in the popular vote. Every year, the semantics of the dispute are recurrent to the point that they have become normalized in public opinion —as a symbolic representation that crystallizes the "public." However, this crystallization does not imply that in the future things will not change; at some point, new horizons of significance of the feminist struggle against presidential power may open up. For the time being, it

---

[9] La Cadera de Eva (2021, Marc 9)

[10] Mondragón (2022, March 9).

[11] Redacción Animal Político (2022, March 5).

can be affirmed that perhaps the only movement that managed to seriously question presidential power in Mexico during the López Obrador administration was undoubtedly the various feminist mobilizations.

References

Ackerman, J. (2020, February 24). Women, go home! *La Jornada*. https://www.jornada.com.mx/2020/02/24/opinion/017a1pol

Aguayo, S. (2020, February 26). On the subject *Reforma*. https://www.reforma.com/sobre-el-sujeto-2020-02-26/op174982

Aguilar, H. (2020, March 11). End of game *Milenio*. https://www.milenio.com/opinion/hector-aguilar-camin/dia-con-dia/fin-de-partida

Albarrán, J. (2020, March 10). We miss them, and we miss them a lot *Milenio*. https://www.milenio.com/opinion/jairo-calixto-albarran/politica-cero/las-extranamos-y-mucho

Anderson, B. (2020, February 24). A day without us is worth $23.4 billion pesos. *Milenio*. https://www.milenio.com/opinion/barbara-anderson/nada-personal-solo-negocios/23-mil-400-mdp-vale-un-dia-sin-nosotras

Animal Político. (2022, February 22). *Better 'men's strike' or women will be tempted to wash dishes at home: Eréndira Sandoval*. Animal Político. https://www.google.com/search?q=traductor&rlz=1C1CHBD_esMX1163MX1163&oq=tr&gs_lcrp=EgZjaHJvbWUq-DggAEEUYJxg7GIAEGIoFMg4IABBFGCcYOxiABBiKBTIGCAEQRRhAMgYIAhBFGD kyDAgDECMYJxiABBiKBTISCAQQABhDGIMBGLEDGIAEGIoFMgYIBRBFGD0yBgg-GEEUYPDIGCAcQRRg80gEIMjQ1MWwowajeoAgCwAgA&sourceid=chrome&ie=UTF-8

Aristegui, C. (2020a, March 13). 8 / 9M - Coronavirus *Reforma*. https://www.reforma.com/8-9m-coronavirus-2020-03-13/op176034

Aristegui, C. (2020b, February 28). Mujeres. *Reforma*. https://www.reforma.com/mujeres-2020-02-28/op175155

Aziz, A. (2020, March 10). AMLO's fall. *El Universal*. https://www.eluniversal.com.mx/opinion/alberto-aziz-nassif/la-bajada-de-amlo/

Baz, V. (2020, February 28). #AdayWithoutUs. *Reforma*. https://www.reforma.com/undiasinnosotras-2020-02-28/op175123

Belaunzarán, F. (2020a, March 10). The day after *Excélsior*. https://www.excelsior.com.mx/opinion/fernando-belaunzaran/el-dia-despues/1368829

Belaunzarán, F. (2020b, February 25). AMLO and the women's strike. *Excélsior*. https://www.excelsior.com.mx/opinion/fernando-belaunzaran/amlo-y-el-paro-de-mujeres/1366048

Bellinghausen, H. (2020, March 2). The march, on the march. *La Jornada*. https://www.jornada.com.mx/2020/03/02/opinion/a08a1cul

Blanco, J. (2020, March 3). Steps to the future. *La Jornada*. https://www.jornada.com.mx/2020/03/03/opinion/017a2pol

Camargo, J. (2020a, March 13). Fearing 9M. *Excélsior*. https://www.excelsior.com.mx/opinion/jorge-camargo/temiendo-al-9m/1369573

Camargo, J. (2020b, February 21). 9M for everyone. *Excélsior*. https://www.excelsior.com.mx/opinion/jorge-camargo/9m-por-todos/1365439

Cárdenas, L. (2020, February 25). Let no one take advantage of the women's movement. *El Universal*. https://www.eluniversal.com.mx/opinion/luis-cardenas/que-nadie-se-aproveche-del-movimiento-de-las-mujeres

Carreño, J. (2020a, March 10). Real events and pseudo-events. *El Universal*. https://www.eluniversal.com.mx/opinion/jose-carreno-carlon/eventos-reales-y-seudoeventos

Carreño, J. (2020b, February 26). Y la culpa no era mía ni de quién se me unía. *El Universal.* https://www.eluniversal.com.mx/opinion/jose-carreno-carlon/y-la-culpa-no-era-mia-ni-de-quien-se-me-unia

Corona, S. (2020, March 5). Mexican ministers promote a national women's strike. *El País.* https://www.google.com/search?q=traductor&rlz=1C1CHBD_esMX1163MX1163&oq=tr&gs_lcrp=EgZjaHJvbWUqDggAEEUYJxg7GIAEGIoFMg4IABBFG-CcYOxiABBiKBTIGCAEQRRhAMgYIAhBFGDkyDAgDECMYJxiABBiKBTISCAQQABhDGIMBGGLEDGIAEGIoFMgYIBRBFGD0yBggGEEUY-PDIGCAcQRRg80gEIMjQ1MWowajeoAgCwAgA&sourceid=chrome&ie=UTF-8

Cossío, J. (2020, February 25). State violence. *El Universal.* https://www.eluniversal.com.mx/opinion/jose-ramon-cossio-diaz/violencia-estatal

Crespo, J. (2020, February 24). López Obrador: acute conspiracyitis. *El Universal.* https://www.eluniversal.com.mx/opinion/jose-antonio-crespo/lopez-obrador-conspiracionitis-aguda

Cueva, Á. (2020a, March 8). The Gender Revolution. *Milenio.* https://www.milenio.com/opinion/alvaro-cueva/ojo-por-ojo/la-revolucion-de-genero

Cueva, Á. (2020b, February 23). AMLO and the national strike. *Milenio.* https://www.milenio.com/opinion/alvaro-cueva/ojo-por-ojo/amlo-y-el-paro-nacional

Díaz, R. (2020, February 23). The "washing dishes" thing was to show how retrograde it is to call on women to hide: Irma Sandoval. *SPD Noticias.* https://www.sdpnoticias.com/nacional/irma-sandoval-lavar-platos-fue-ironia-para-exhibir-retrogado-de-paro.html

Dresser, D. (2020, February 24). Marching and stopping. *Reforma.* https://www.reforma.com/marchar-y-parar-2020-02-24/op174841

Esquinca, V. (2020, March 8). There was no way. *Excélsior.* https://www.excelsior.com.mx/opinion/vianey-esquinca/no-hubo-manera/1368525

Fernández de Cevallos, D. (2020, March 9). La rebelión de las musas. *Milenio.* https://www.milenio.com/opinion/diego-fernandez-de-cevallos/sin-rodeos/la-rebelion-de-las-musas

Fuentes, M. (2020, March 9). Hoy nueve, ninguna se mueve. *Excélsior.* https://www.excelsior.com.mx/opinion/mario-luis-fuentes/hoy-nueve-ninguna-se-mueve/1368668

Galván, E. (2020a, February 25). Money. *La Jornada.* https://www.jornada.com.mx/2020/02/25/opinion/006o1eco

Galván, E. (2020b, February 29). Money. Women's opinion on the women's strike. *La Jornada.* https://www.jornada.com.mx/2020/02/29/opinion/008o1eco

Galván, E. (2020c, March 5). Money. *La Jornada.* https://www.jornada.com.mx/2020/03/05/opinion/006o1eco

Galván, E. (2020d, March 6). What's next after 9M? *La Jornada.* https://www.jornada.com.mx/2020/03/06/opinion/006o1eco

Galván, E. (2020e, March 9). Women's Day: Yesterday the march, today the strike. *La Jornada.* https://www.jornada.com.mx/2020/03/09/opinion/010o1eco

Gamés, G. (2020, February 24). The blind eye. *Milenio.* https://www.milenio.com/opinion/gil-games/uno-hasta-el-fondo/la-vista-gorda_2

García, S. (2020a, March 7). El presidente que no quiso defender a las mujeres. *El Universal.* https://www.eluniversal.com.mx/opinion/salvador-garcia-soto/el-presidente-que-no-quiso-defender-las-mujeres

García, S. (2020b, March 9). A Monday without women and with weak weight. *El Universal.* https://www.eluniversal.com.mx/opinion/salvador-garcia-soto/un-lunes-sin-mujeres-y-con-el-peso-debil

Garfias, F. (2020, February 25). Soft blow against AMLO. *Excélsior.* https://www.excelsior.com.mx/opinion/francisco-garfias/golpe-blando-contra-amlo/1366042

Gasman, N. (2020, March 10). Thunder and silence. *La Jornada.* https://www.jornada.com.mx/2020/03/10/opinion/008a1pol

Gómez, L. (2020a, March 10). Polarization that serves. *Milenio.* https://www.milenio.com/opinion/leopoldo-gomez/tercer-grado/polarizacion-que-sirve

Gómez, L. (2020b, March 3). Beyond march 9. *Milenio.* https://www.milenio.com/opinion/leopoldo-gomez/tercer-grado/mas-alla-del-9-de-marzo

González, A. (2020a, February 28). From 'conservatism' with a woman's face to fakeminism. *El Universal.* https://www.eluniversal.com.mx/opinion/ariel-gonzalez/del-conservadurismo-con-rostro-de-mujer-al-fakeminismo

González, Á. (2020b, March 15). Sorority. *La Jornada.* https://www.jornada.com.mx/2020/03/15/opinion/024a1cap.

Gordillo, G. (2020, March 7). Fly, fly sea witches. *La Jornada.* https://www.jornada.com.mx/2020/03/07/opinion/019a1eco

Güemes, C. (2020, March 10). Women of fire, women of snow. *El Universal.* https://www.eluniversal.com.mx/opinion/cesar-guemes/mujeres-de-fuego-mujeres-de-nieve

Hernández, J. (2020a, March 10). Astillero. La Jornada. https://www.jornada.com.mx/2020/03/10/opinion/016o1pol

Hernández, J. (2020b, February 21). Astillero. *La Jornada.* https://www.jornada.com.mx/2020/02/21/opinion/008o1pol

Hernández, J. (2020c, February 24). Astillero. *La Jornada.* https://www.jornada.com.mx/2020/02/24/opinion/008o1pol

Hernández, J. (2020d, March 5). Astillero. *La Jornada.* https://www.jornada.com.mx/2020/03/05/opinion/008o1pol

Hernández, J. (2020e, March 6). Astillero. *La Jornada.* https://www.jornada.com.mx/2020/03/06/opinion/008o1pol

Hernández, J. (2020f, March 9). Astillero. *La Jornada.* https://www.jornada.com.mx/2020/03/09/opinion/012o1pol

Homs, R. (2020, March 7). The Cardinal's statements. *El Universal.* https://www.eluniversal.com.mx/opinion/ricardo-homs/las-declaraciones-del-cardenal

Infobae. (2020, March 4). "I didn't even realize it": López Obrador will postpone the start of the sale of tickets for the airplane raffle after criticism from feminist organizations. *Infobae.* https://www.infobae.com/america/mexico/2020/03/04/se-ofenden-lopez-obrador-postergara-el-inicio-de-la-venta-de-cachitos-para-la-rifa-del-avion-tras-criticas-de-organizaciones-feministas/

Jardínez, R. (2020, February 21). Be careful... now conservatives call themselves feminists: AMLO. *WRadio.* https://wradio.com.mx/radio/2020/02/21/nacional/1582314057_025610.html

Jáuregui, M. (2020a, February 24). External danger. *Reforma.* https://www.reforma.com/peligro-externo-2020-02-24/op174845

Jáuregui, M. (2020b, February 27). 9M unstoppable. *Reforma.* https://www.reforma.com/9m-imparable-2020-02-27/op175045

La Cadera de Eva. (2021, Marc 9). "On the 9th, no one moves," women join the national strike. *La Cadera de Eva.* https://lacaderadeeva.com/actualidad/el-nueve-nadie-se-mueve-mujeres-se-suman-al-paro-nacional/2834

La Jornada. (2020a, March 3). Women: A historic strike. *La Jornada.* https://www.jornada.com.mx/2020/03/10/opinion/002a1edi

La Jornada. (2020b, March 6). Women: Equality and an end to violence. *La Jornada.* https://www.jornada.com.mx/2020/03/06/opinion/002a1edi

Linares, L. (2020a, February 26). Marches and absence. *La Jornada.* https://www.jornada.com.mx/2020/02/26/opinion/017a2pol.

Linares, L. (2020b, March 11). Background and crisis. *La Jornada.* https://www.jornada.com.mx/2020/03/11/opinion/017a2pol

Loaeza, G. (2020, March 5). Sunday 8 and Monday 9. *Reforma.* https://www.reforma.com/domingo-8-y-lunes-9-2020-03-05/op175494

Lomnitz, C. (2020, March 4). Women's protest matters more. *La Jornada.* https://www.jornada.com.mx/2020/03/04/opinion/017a2pol

López Dóriga, J. (2020, March 10). For the president, a perfect storm. *Milenio.* https://www.milenio.com/opinion/joaquin-lopez-doriga/en-privado/para-el-presidente-tormenta-perfecta

Lozano, G. (2020, February 25). Two worlds in conflict *Reforma.* https://www.reforma.com/dos-mundos-en-pugna-2020-02-25/op174946

Malvido, A. (2020, March 10). March 8 and 9 with jacarandas. *El Universal.* https://www.eluniversal.com.mx/opinion/adriana-malvido/el-8-y-el-9-de-marzo-con-jacarandas

Marín, C. (2020a, March 10). 'Adversaries' everywhere. *Milenio.* https://www.milenio.com/opinion/carlos-marin/el-asalto-la-razon/adversarios-por-doquier

Marín, C. (2020b, March 5). A real 'witch' hunt. *Milenio.* https://www.milenio.com/opinion/carlos-marin/el-asalto-la-razon/una-verdadera-caceria-de-brujas

Martínez, C. (2020, March 11). Y retembló en sus centros la tierra. *La Jornada.* https://www.jornada.com.mx/2020/03/11/opinion/016a1pol

Maza, V. (2020, February 22). Gender unity to save us from barbarism. *Milenio.* https://www.milenio.com/opinion/veronica-maza-bustamante/el-sexodromo/unidad-de-genero-para-salvarnos-de-la-barbarie

Melgar, I. (2020, February 22). A day without us. *Excélsior.* https://www.excelsior.com.mx/opinion/ivonne-melgar/un-dia-sin-nosotras/1365604

Mondragón, L. M. (2022, March 9). The nine, nobody moves. *Cámara.* https://comunicacionsocial.diputados.gob.mx/revista/index.php/a-profundidad/el-nueve-nadie-se-mueve

Monreal, R. (2020, March 10). 8-9M: What days! *Milenio.* https://www.milenio.com/opinion/ricardo-monreal-avila/antilogia/8-9m-que-dias

Muñoz, G. (2020, February 29). Those from below. Women's strike on March 9. *La Jornada.* https://www.jornada.com.mx/2020/02/29/opinion/012o1pol

Nacif, B. (2020, March 10). La democracia, en deuda con las mujeres. *El Universal.* https://www.eluniversal.com.mx/opinion/benito-nacif/la-democracia-en-deuda-con-las-mujeres

Nájar, A. (2020, February 21). The Fátima case: How AMLO'S response to femicides became a crisis for his government. *BBC News Mundo.* https://www.bbc.com/mundo/noticias-america-latina-51583486

Ordorica, A. (2020, February 26). Only AMLO cares about Mexico. *El Universal.* https://www.eluniversal.com.mx/opinion/ana-paula-ordorica/solo-amlo-se-preocupa-por-mexico.

Orozco, S. (2020, March 5). Marchar y parar. *Reforma.* https://www.reforma.com/marchar-y-parar-2020-03-05/op175491

Peredo, X. (2020a, March 10). What happened yesterday? *Reforma.* https://www.reforma.com/aplicaciones/editoriales/editorial.aspx?id=175821

Peredo, X. (2020b, February 29). I see a light. *Reforma.* https://www.reforma.com/veo-una-luz-2020-02-29/op175209

Puig, C. (2020a, February 25). To avoid #pinkwashing. *Milenio.* https://www.milenio.com/opinion/carlos-puig/duda-razonable/para-evitar-el-pinkwashing

Puig, C. (2020b, March 2). Women, the virus and the 4T. *Millennium.* https://www.milenio.com/opinion/carlos-puig/duda-razonable/las-mujeres-el-virus-y-la-4t

Ramírez, P. (2020, March 6). Feministas de papel. *El Universal.* https://www.eluniversal.com.mx/opinion/peniley-ramirez/fem inistas-de-papel

Raphael, R. (2020a, March 9). It's the revolution of the century. *El Universal.* https://www.eluniversal.com.mx/opinion/ricardo-raphael/es-la-revolucion-del-siglo

Raphael, R. (2020b, February 24). La culpa es de Las Brujas del Mar. *El Universal.* https://www.eluniversal.com.mx/opinion/ricardo-raphael/la-culpa-es-de-las-brujas-del-mar

Redacción Animal Político. (2022, March 5). Ahead of the #8M feminist march, authorities seal off the National Palace and other Mexico City buildings. Animal Político. https://www.google.com/search?q=traductor&rlz=1C1CHBD_esMX1163MX1163&oq=tr&gs_lcrp=EgZjaHJvbWUqDggAEEUYJxg7GIAEGIoFMg4IABBFGCcYOxiABBiKBTIGCAEQRRhAMgYIAhBFGDkyDAgDECMYJxiABBiKBTISCAQQABhDGIMBGGGLEDGIAEGIoFMgYIBRBFGD0yBggGEEUYPDIGCAcQRRg80gEIMjQ1MWowajeoAgCwAgA&sourceid=chrome&ie=UTF-8

Redacción El Universal. (2020, February 21). After calling for "A Day Without Women," Beatriz Gutiérrez says #NoToTheNationalStrike. *El Universal.* https://www.google.com/search?q=traductor&rlz=1C1CHBD_esMX1163MX1163&oq=tr&gs_lcrp=EgZjaHJvbWUqDggAEEUYJxg7GIAEGIoFMg4IABBFGCcYOxiABBiKBTIGCAEQRRhAMgYIAhBFGD

kyDAgDECMYJxiABBiKBTISCAQQABhDGIMBGLEDGIAEGIoFMgYIBRBFGD0yBgg-GEEUYPDIGCAcQRRg80gEIMjQ1MWowajeoAgCwAgA&sourceid=chrome&ie=UTF-8

Revueltas, R. (2020, February 23). *El poder de las mujeres.* Milenio. https://www.milenio.com/opinion/roman-revueltas-retes/la-semana-de-roman-revueltas-retes/el-poder-de-las-mujeres

Rodríguez, R. (2020a, February 22). El botín político de la violencia de género. *El Universal.* https://www.eluniversal.com.mx/opinion/raul-rodriguez-cortes/el-botin-politico-de-la-violencia-de-genero

Rodríguez, R. (2020b, March 6). Women will stop despite the troglodytes. *El Universal.* https://www.eluniversal.com.mx/opinion/raul-rodriguez-cortes/las-mujeres-pararan-pesar-de-los-trogloditas

Romero, J. (2020a, February 28). It's a strike and it's a warning. *Excélsior.* https://www.excelsior.com.mx/opinion/jose-elias-romero-apis/es-un-paro-y-es-una-advertencia/1366815

Romero, J. (2020b, March 6). A day of women and a day without women. *Excélsior.* https://www.excelsior.com.mx/opinion/jose-elias-romero-apis/un-dia-de-mujeres-y-un-dia-sin-mujeres/1368208

Rubinstein, J. (2020, February 28). No more days without women. *El Universal.* https://www.eluniversal.com.mx/opinion/jose-rubinstein/no-mas-dias-sin-mujeres.

Sarmiento, S. (2020, February 25). Fakeministas. *Reforma.* https://www.reforma.com/fakeministas-2020-02-25/op174943

Sefcovich, S. (2020, March 1). Is it the same government? *El Universal.* https://www.eluniversal.com.mx/opinion/sara-sefchovich/es-el-mismo-gobierno

Woldenberg, J. (2020a, March 1). With me or against me. *El Universal.* https://www.eluniversal.com.mx/opinion/jose-woldenberg/conmigo-o-contra-mi

Woldenberg, J. (2020b, March 3). Equal rights and no to violence. *El Universal.* https://www.eluniversal.com.mx/opinion/jose-woldenberg/igualdad-de-derechos-y-no-la-violencia

Yañez, B. (2020, February 26). The national women's strike is a non-partisan demand, say Sea Witches. *Política Expansión.* https://politica.expansion.mx/sociedad/2020/02/26/el-paro-nacional-de-mujeres-es-un-reclamo-sin-partidos-aseguran-brujas-del-mar

Zamarrón, H. (2020, March 1). The patriarchy is going to fall. *Milenio.* https://www.milenio.com/opinion/hector-zamarron/afinidades-selectivas/el-patriarcado-se-va-a-caer

Chapter 7
Conclusion

Abstract In this book, we have shown how presidential power, feminist mobilizations, and public opinion in Mexico were related in the early 2020s. This relationship was particularly novel due to a political context favorable to the expression of progressive social demands. The first leftist government to gain presidential power appeared particularly sensitive to the demonstrations that for years had been demanding effective policies to stop femicide and violence against women. However, the president translated the feminist demonstrations as expressions intended to undermine the legitimacy of his government and his Fourth Transformation project. Even when criticisms were leveled at the mayor of Mexico City, they served to question the legitimacy of the president. The relationship between feminist mobilizations and the officialism established since 2018 was tense, and it generated processes of meaning making about what such mobilizations represent, what authentic feminism was, and how both expressions should be aligned in the face of presidential power. Public opinion echoed these disputes over meaning.

Keywords Feminist mobilizations · Presidential power · Public opinion · Civil repair · Civil mobilization · Anti-civil mobilization

The #MeToo movement in Mexico expanded rapidly in 2018 as a means to denounce harassment against women in workspaces of all kinds and particularly in higher education institutions, for example, clotheslines denouncing the violence were a common practice in universities across the country. Mexican public opinion constructed a narrative of support and criticism of #MeToo that reproduced, to a certain extent, the debate at the international level unleashed between *#MeToo* and *Autre Parole*. Thus, class position, the way in which relationships between men and women are perceived (asymmetrically or symmetrically), the boundaries that distinguish between harassment and seduction, whether complaints are anonymous, and whether the presumption of innocence of the alleged harasser could all be considered purifying or contaminating elements, in other words, civil or anti-civil.

L. A. Cardona Acuña, N. Arteaga Botello, *Feminism, Power and Public Opinion in Mexico*, SpringerBriefs in Sociology,
https://doi.org/10.1007/978-3-032-14141-5_7

However, two new homologies were added to the Mexican dispute between civil and anti-civil within the *#MeToo* movement: (1) punishment as an act of justice or revenge and (2) women as heroes or villains. While these two innovations reflected a particular meaning-making process, the themes of eroticism and sexuality prominent in the international *#MeToo* and *Autre Parole* debate were absent.

The introduction of presidential power into the *#MeToo* debate—challenged by the appointment of an ambassador to Panama—caused the elements of class and status to be further branded. The president charged that *#MeToo* was a movement of the middle and upper classes, not the popular classes; therefore, that situated it as an impure expression. Similarly, the president connected the women who mobilized against his ambassadorial appointment with populist discourse, so they were accused of being conservatives. On the other hand, he emphasized that even if there was no legally established harassment complaint against the person he appointed as ambassador, the accusations violated the presumption of innocence of the alleged harasser, inciting his lynching and not the exercise of justice. This response from the president was echoed by some members of the public that supported him; at the same time, it also unleashed critics who questioned his interpretation of what harassment means and the values of the women who denounce. Each of the positions that crystallized within public opinion generated narratives with plots aimed at positioning the president and #MeToo as morally civil and anti-civil actors. In doing so, they constructed horizons of legitimacy and illegitimacy in defining presidential power and #MeToo, as well as two perspectives on what social inclusion and civil solidarity mean.

Public opinion also served as a sounding board for feminist mobilizations in which the system of classification of actors who supported or questioned the legitimacy of such mobilizations was exposed. In the case of the #NMCMV, public opinion again activated the binary system of symbolic attribution. Social class, age, the type of demand or sanction sought, the political affiliation of the conveners, as well as the relationship with presidential power, all went into the puzzle of the narratives wielded to define the civil or anti-civil character of #NMCMV. In this case, it is worth highlighting that contaminating references to class or age were differentially activated within public opinion. Social class was activated as a discrediting referent by groups critical of the mobilization, while age was employed by those in favor; both were central components in the dispute between #MeToo and *Autre Parole*.

Notably, the competition over controlling the meaning of the mobilization based on class and age established a difference on how to categorize the civil and anti-civil character of #NMCMV. The competition over meaning was different from the #MeToo mobilization, and it also differed from the national strike analyzed in Chap. 6. With respect to the strike, social class returned to bear central weight in the classification of purity and impurity of the movement, as did the link to presidential power. Also, present was the classification system based on the type of demands, denunciations, and, above all, the attribution of conservative and progressive leanings to the women who called for the #NMCMV mobilization. The classification system also highlighted a racial imputation: if white women were supporting the movement, then the call for the strike should be labeled as illegitimate and inauthentic. In this way, an element present in the dispute between #MeToo and *Autre Parole* was brought to account: whiteness as a contaminating attribution, much in the same way that, as discussed above, age was assumed as an element of impurity for those who criticized positions close to presidential power.

These criteria of attribution defining civil and anti-civil characteristic to mobilization and feminism in the 2020s in Mexico reveal a social effort, reflected by public opinion, to define who and what can be the authentic and inauthentic voices and collective manifestations. Feminist demands and those of other women's groups appeared patterned by attributes that had little or nothing to do with the demands for addressing femicide and violence against women. The demands to respond to these damaging phenomena, aimed at guaranteeing social inclusion and broadening social solidarity, were subject to the evaluation of who speaks and mobilizes public opinion.

The patterns of civil anti-civil classification towards feminist expressions and mobilizations, as we have seen, are not instances, articulations, or narratives disconnected from one another. Nor can it be said that they are meanings with an unrepeatable spatial and temporal specificity. The attributions constantly and consistently made by public opinion have been shown as expressions of collective representations anchored deep in the cultural structure of Mexican society. Collective representations are based on organized systems of narrative structures in which social actors are emplaced in events and plots. Above all, they assign to each actor a particular moral responsibility, with the capacity to produce positive or negative effects on society, with agency qualified as moral, rational, and strategically oriented, but more importantly, they define the actors involved as exemplary models of both civil virtue and civil vice.

In this book, we have also highlighted that the newspapers in which the different positions on presidential power and feminist mobilizations were expressed were pluralistic in almost all respects. This pluralism allows us to affirm that, although there were patterns of criticism in certain newspapers, particularly *Reforma*, against presidential power and in favor of the demonstrations or #MeToo movements, there were also arguments that favored presidential power and criticized some mobilizations. The clearest example of the latter is the newspaper La *Jornada*. However, at times, the newspapers coincided in certain opinions, for example, *Reforma* and *La Jornada*, as well as *La Jornada* and *Excélsior*, two newspapers totally distanced along the political spectrum. Certainly, what they all agreed on was the diagnosis of harassment, violence against women, and femicide. They affirmed that these phenomena are the result of a complex structural process that must be addressed in a radical and profound manner. The set of newspapers we analyzed also proposed similar solutions to the problems faced by women in Mexico. The differences emerged when the plot narratives of the actors on the social and political chessboard were established. However, disagreements were evident not only among the newspapers but also within them.

Importantly, public opinion operates as a meta-narrative about the events occurring in a society, and in this book, we have revealed its contours in the Mexican case. Its effects were not only symbolic; they also generated dynamics of action and drove the modification of institutions and even laws, having a profound impact on people's lives. This case has allowed us to understand how society—through certain communicative institutions, such as the press or public opinion surveys, understands or interprets its relationships, its institutions, presidential power, and social mobilization. It is through public opinion that we have shown the echoes of the different productions of meaning generated by diverse actors. When we explored those productions of meaning, it was possible to observe how there was a dynamic structure or a system of symbols that Mexican society shares. This system is connected to other systems of meaning, as we could observe in the debate between *#MeToo* and *Autre Parole,* activated to give meaning to the world of politics and to the processes of communicative interaction.

In this sense, by proposing an analysis such as the one carried out for this book, we do not see social life as a mere world plagued by rational, greedy, and selfish actors who strive only to achieve stark personal interests of social meaning. A vision that depicts social reality as a game of *realpolitik* can only result in a distorted perception of reality in which all its actors contribute to a constant degradation of the bonds of social inclusion and solidarity. We believe that, despite the imposition of *realpolitik* as a common image of social life, the truth is that people continue to create meanings, and both meaning and emotion remain important. Cultural sociology, including civil sphere theory, has allowed us to achieve our goals for the book: to study how public opinion creates meanings in the context of feminist mobilizations that confront presidential power. Crucially, this confrontation is constantly elaborated through cultural referents that are at the same time patterned and contingent.

Within public opinion, it can be observed how class, race, age, and proximity to presidential power serve as references to establish the degree of probity or contamination of actors and institutions. It should not be forgotten that public opinion is a symbolic representation that condenses the idea of the "public" as if it expressed a structure of shared feelings that confront society. Social actors appeal to public opinion as a normative referent of civil discourse. It is precisely in this space, in which feminist mobilizations and presidential power were assumed as democratic, in which both sides accused each other of having fractured public morality, and in which presidential power was supported or criticized, either for not creating or for creating dynamics of inclusion and solidarity. It is in the space of public opinion in which the binary system of classification of civil discourse and the institutional domains of presidential power is mediated. It is in this mediation that the feeling of democratic life of the country was structured. As it happens in democratic societies, it is not possible to find a consensual agreement within public opinion on the issues debated in society and politics, because the meaning that is socially constructed on solidarity and inclusion varies according to the moral attributions that social actors make to each other.

Unlike in feminist and gender studies, this book shows that feminist demands, and their justifications create disputes through communication. In the civil sphere, this communication mobilizes the idea that women are capable of confronting violence as heroes who resist and fight, thereby transforming their environment and generating consensus on the despicable and reprehensible nature of these attacks.

This work complements the findings of gender studies, by showing that moral debates about violence against women or gender-based violence are symbolic acts open to interpretation and that public opinion (re)interprets cultural structures. In this way, our work sheds light on how significant changes can be promoted culturally to expand social solidarity in favor of women and against gender violence. In contrast to feminist studies, it shows that "economic causes" or "heteropatriarchal structures" only become relevant political elements of symbolic dispute and controversy in society if public opinion considers them to be so within the civil/anti-civil binary system.

This book represents a contribution to understanding a particular dynamic of Mexican society in the 2020s. It sheds light on the possibility of understanding how power dynamics are constructed from vantage point of civil sphere theory. As Reed (2023) suggests, for cultural sociology to consolidate, it is necessary to account for the power processes at play in the competition for meaning that actors put into play in the face of events considered morally relevant. However, it must be borne in mind that this accounting is only possible if there is no conflation between power and efficient cause, in other words, if we stop believing that power is only such when it is the cause of things remaining the same or changing. Power is not a fixed social structure that generates pre-defined results, but rather a process in which the actors assume that they have force given to them by their symbolic understanding of their reality and their relationship with other individuals or groups of individuals. It is precisely this meaning of the concept of power that can provide broader interpretative horizons for understanding social processes.

What can be observed in this book is precisely how both the presidential power and the actors behind the feminist mobilizations managed to establish their strength in a system of significance within public opinion—as a structure of feelings that appeals to a civil normative referent. Each of the actors brought to light in this book thus put their power at stake, giving rise to the consideration that what is at stake are democratic institutions. The result, like any democratic game, is not zero-sum, and in our case, it shows how the competition for the meaning of feminist mobilizations and presidential power allowed the dynamic creation of meaning about the significance of a broad set of issues surrounding violence against women and femicide. In the background, these processes of creation of meaning allow us to understand the ways in which Mexican public opinion imagines the construction of democracy.

Reference

Reed, I. A. (2023). *Sociology as Human Science. Essays on interpretation and causal pluralism.* Palgrave Macmillan.

GPSR Compliance
The European Union's (EU) General Product Safety Regulation (GPSR) is a set
of rules that requires consumer products to be safe and our obligations to
ensure this.

If you have any concerns about our products, you can contact us on

ProductSafety@springernature.com

In case Publisher is established outside the EU, the EU authorized
representative is:

Springer Nature Customer Service Center GmbH
Europaplatz 3
69115 Heidelberg, Germany